AF263657

DEFYING APARTHEID

BY MANJU SONI

Defying Apartheid

First Print Edition: October 2021

Published by NUMA LLC.
CT, 06355

Cover design: Andrea@AndreaHo.com, Streetlight Graphics

ISBN-978-0-9977196-1-1

PART 1

1

JULY 1968 BEGAN LIKE ANY winter month in the small Eastern Cape town of Stutterheim in South Africa, with windy days, occasional rain, and lots of sunshine.

The town nestles at the foot of the Amathole Mountains, which means "calves" in native Xhosa. In a few months, the humpback whales with their shiny and sleek babies would travel from the cold waters of False Bay in the south, to the warm waters of the Indian Ocean farther north. In the town itself, built around the pretty Lutheran church with its Cape Dutch gables, the townspeople of Stutterheim went about their business. The baker knew all his customers by name, and the barber greeted his with a friendly nod and asked how their children were doing in school. It was a caring, loving community.

It was, however, for whites only.

The central pillar of apartheid policy was the Population Registration Act of 1950, which categorized every citizen of the total population of twenty-two million into white or nonwhite. Nonwhites (or blacks, as they preferred to be called) were subdivided into Africans, coloureds (people of mixed descent) and Indians (people whose ancestors came either willingly or were brought as virtual slaves from India).

Africans made up 66 percent of the population, with whites, coloureds, and Indians making up 20, 11, and 3 percent, respectively. Every aspect of life under apartheid was rigidly triaged and funded according to population group, with whites at the top and Africans at the bottom; in between were Indians and coloureds.

The second pillar of apartheid legislation was the Group Areas Act, under which the different racial groups were geographically separated. Whites were housed in the pristine northern suburbs of a city or town, and the three black groups lived on the southern side, each in its own separate area.

Stutterheim was no different. A few miles away from the white town, in the adjacent shantytown, African men gulped down their coffees and thick slices of brown bread as wood smoke curled up into the dark sky. By four in the morning, they stood in line, wearing little more than their threadbare pants, worn-out shoes, frayed shirts, and tired gray jackets, waiting for white farmers to come by and pick them up for the day's work. They chatted softly and blew warm air into their hands. Some coughed, and others took a step or two back, afraid to get tuberculosis. It was winter, and work was scarce; no one could afford to fall sick.

Some went into town looking for work. But the town council had passed a law requiring all nonwhites obtain permits to stay longer than seventy-two hours, making day labor the only option.

It was little more than three years since Nelson Mandela, 'Accused Number 1', captivated the courtroom at the end of his treason trial. The forty-six-year-old boxer, tall and regal, outlined his rationale for resorting to an armed struggle against apartheid.

"I do not deny that I planned sabotage… I planned it as a result of a calm and sober assessment of the political situation that had arisen after many years of tyranny, exploitation, and oppression of my people by the whites."

In his steady voice, he went on to admit that after the Sharpeville Massacre, when police killed sixty-nine peaceful protesters in a hail of bullets that lasted only forty seconds, he and his colleagues founded Umkhonto we Sizwe (Spear of the Nation), the armed wing of his liberation movement, the African National Congress (ANC).

The crowd listened attentively as Mandela concluded, "Above all, we want equal political rights… I know this sounds revolutionary to whites in this country, because the majority of voters will be Africans… But this fear cannot be allowed to stand in the way of the only solution that will guarantee racial harmony and freedom for all.

"During my lifetime I have dedicated myself to this struggle of the African people. I have fought against white domination, and I have fought against black domination. I have cherished the ideal of a democratic and free society, in which all persons live together in harmony and with equal opportunities. It is an ideal that I hope to live for and to achieve. But if need be, it is an ideal for which I am prepared to die."

When the judge announced his verdict, the accused—six African, one Indian, and one white—escaped the gallows but were sentenced to life in prison. The single white prisoner was sent to a whites-only prison, while the black prisoners were incarcerated in an island prison surrounded by shark-infested waters out in the Atlantic Ocean—Robben Island. Not only did the government imprison Mandela; but it also tried to wipe out every trace of him by making it illegal to display his image or quote him.

Mandela's fellow freedom fighter, Oliver Tambo, evaded capture and fled the country. Their movement, the ANC, and its ally, the South African Communist Party (SACP), already banned, went underground. Anyone caught displaying the flags, or in any other way promoting these organizations, was arrested.

But by the time Mandela reached Robben Island, Tambo, a science and math teacher turned lawyer, had already begun to resurrect the ANC in exile.

Since then the country had returned to relative calm.

There was a new leader in power in the government. B. J. Vorster was the fourth prime minister of South Africa under apartheid. A large barrel-chested man with thick eyebrows and piercing blue eyes, Vorster was elected to office when his predecessor,

Hendrik Verwoerd, the "grand wizard" of apartheid, was assassinated.

The son of a successful sheep farmer, Vorster studied law at Stellenbosch University. During World War II, he joined a pro-Nazi group, the Ossewabrandwag (Ox-wagon Sentinel), to fight against the British, who had defeated his people during the Anglo-Boer Wars fifty years before.

The Ossewabrandwag was responsible for many acts of sabotage, for which Vorster was arrested and thrown into solitary confinement. Released after two years, he joined the Afrikaner Broederbond (Afrikaner Brotherhood), a white-supremacist body.

The puritanical Broederbond limited its membership to white males, twenty-five or older, who spoke Afrikaans and belonged to one of the Afrikaner churches. All were handpicked, and most were professional citizens in positions of power who had been watched secretly for years before being offered membership. The membership ceremony involved an altar on which a fake body with a dagger in its heart lay in a shroud. A priest chanted, "He who betrays the Bond will be destroyed by the Bond. The Bond never forgets."

By 1947, the Broederbond had developed its policy of total segregation for South Africa and its planned takeover of the country from its British rulers. Changes favoring rural areas where Afrikaners were in the majority were made to electoral boundaries. Broederbond members took up key government positions and sidelined English-speaking bureaucrats and soldiers.

The 1948 elections were the Broederbond's hour of greatest triumph. A small band of "brothers" in 1918, they had painstakingly infiltrated key organizations and seized power of the country.

Three beliefs were at the core of Vorster's philosophy. The first was his firm conviction that South Africa really belonged only to the white race. The basis of this was his understanding that when his Dutch ancestors arrived on the southern tip of Africa, none of the multitude of African tribes had officially laid claim to the land. Thus, in his eyes, it was perfectly acceptable that whites owned 93 percent of the land, even though they were only 20 percent of the population.

His second belief was that white people, both his countrymen and those in the rest of the world, would always stand with other white people against blacks. He also knew that if he played upon their fears of communism, it would be easier to get them to side with him.

Last, he was an ardent believer in the superiority of whites. He didn't believe blacks capable of orchestrating an effective freedom struggle. Instead, in his mind they were puppets of white activists, whom he regarded as the ultimate traitors to class and race. This thinking permeated all aspects of his government and, in fact, much of white society at the time.

But that winter of 1968, unknown to Vorster, a gap-toothed nineteen-year-old African student was in Stutterheim, planning to turn his thinking on its head.

2

STEPHEN BANTU BIKO, A STRAPPING young man of six-foot-two with a gravelly voice and penetrating eyes, looked around and assessed the crowd of a few hundred students scattered at tables around the church hall. About half the students were black. It was the United Christian Movement (UCM) conference.

He was in his second year at the University of Natal's non-European section, the only black medical school in the country, out of a total of seven.

A few years before, as a freshman medical student, Steve Biko's charisma got him elected to the student representative council of the medical school. As such, he automatically became a member of NUSAS (National Union of South African Students), a liberal university student group in which white students outnumbered blacks eight to one.

A good number of the white students in NUSAS were heirs of wealthy families of industry. To many of them, being a member of NUSAS was a resumé-filler to get a major scholarship or a place at Oxford. They were preoccupied with issues affecting whites, and they expected blacks to fit in. They held their parties in residences where black students were not allowed, and at national student conferences; they easily accepted segregated accommodations, casually dismissing black students' objections.

At his first NUSAS conference two years before, Biko and fellow black students had requested that the national flag not be flown in the conference hall. Blacks were by law not allowed to even touch the flag, and to them it celebrated the oppression of the black man. But they were outvoted.

The next year, NUSAS held its conference at the prestigious whites-only Rhodes University. Biko and his friends had expected to stay on the campus, but they were told the conference was to be segregated. African, Indian, and coloured students could not stay in the residences. It was the turning point for him.

He made a motion that the conference adjourn until a more suitable venue was found, and was surprised at the heated debate that broke out. He then suggested that white students come to stay with black students in the black housing areas. His offer was received with stunned silence. Many white students became irritated with him for pushing an issue that couldn't be changed easily.

The debate at Rhodes had lasted hours, and by the time the vote was taken, the sun was rising, and the issue of where to sleep had become moot. As he expected, white students won the vote.

Biko didn't blame white students for their feeling of superiority. From birth, they were taught of their elevated place in society and indeed in the world. It was simply the way they were brought up. They couldn't begin to imagine what it was like to be black in apartheid South Africa.

They tended to take blacks for granted, expecting them to accept their second class status, to be patient, and to move things along gradually, from within the existing system.

Now many black students, having fled NUSAS, joined the newly formed church-oriented UCM. But again, the conference was being held in a white town, and this time, to add insult to injury, black students were expected to apply for a permit to stay longer than seventy-two hours. Biko had had enough.

His only hesitation was that many of the same white students were his friends—working-class people who were dedicated activists, people he joked around with and respected. They had accomplished a coup of sorts two years before when they succeeded in getting Robert Kennedy to visit South Africa. Biko feared losing their friendship, but he was determined to make his point.

The crowd hushed as he cleared his throat and began to read the motion.

"To express our disagreement with the issue of the seventy-two-hour clause in the Group Areas Act, which forces black students at this conference to apply for a permit to stay in the town, I present a motion to not observe the rule at all. Black students should stay in the town of Stutterheim for as long as the conference is open."

The hall was silent for a few seconds, and then a loud buzz broke out. Everyone had an opinion and was making it known. He watched as the organizers tried in vain to restore calm.

Some students agreed with the motion while others proposed a symbolic walkout from the town, across the town's border, followed by a return to continue the conference.

He waited for a lull in the noise and then stated loudly, "If the police arrest anyone, it will be us black students only. We black students will allow ourselves to be arrested. But you, the white students here, should protest our arrest."

"How should we protest your arrest? Are you suggesting we cause a disturbance and run the risk of being arrested ourselves?" a young woman in the audience yelled.

"You should protest the arrests through a non-violent protest tactic like that used by Gandhi. When the vans come to collect us, whites should lie down in front of them and refuse to move," he said.

Most of the white students disagreed. They felt the suggestion was irresponsible and radical. He was not surprised, being arrested was too extreme a step for them, with possible impact on their careers.

One young man called out, "This is bullshit. You're dividing the student body."

Biko replied, "And you're introducing *baaskaap* (hierarchy)."

He watched the tide turn against him as some of the undecided black students began to side with the white students. He was disappointed but not entirely surprised. It was time to bring out his backup plan.

"This clause affects the black students only. The decision to vote therefore depends on us. We blacks will have a separate meeting to discuss this."

The organizers, keen not to see the conference derailed, eagerly agreed.

The next day, at the meeting of black students, Biko launched into the main proposal he had been planning for weeks. "We have to get out of this mentality of taking the backseat in our own battle. It's like expecting the slave to work with the slave master's son to get rid of slavery. I propose we break away and form our own student group, but one for blacks only."

Some students didn't really understand the thinking behind the radical plan he was proposing. They continued with their argument for walking across the border and returning.

Biko patiently explained that the issue was not the seventy-two-hour clause. It was the larger one of who should be driving the struggle against the black man's oppression: blacks or whites? "To me, it's not acceptable that whites are our oppressors, and they are also our saviors."

A number of students were concerned. There were too few black university students in the country to make a blacks-only organization viable. Belonging to NUSAS and UCM brought a certain amount of leverage.

"I don't agree," said a female student. "It's playing straight into government's hands. They want to divide us, and a blacks-only organization will do just that. It goes against the very spirit of non-racialism."

"Let's be honest, non-racialism has not worked. As long as we blacks are suffering from our inferiority complexes, we will be useless as co-architects of a normal society, where we are nothing else but people for our own sake," Biko replied.

To his relief, after another few hours of furious discussion, the students finally voted to form a breakaway blacks-only organization once the conference was over. They then returned to the conference and agreed to walk symbolically across the border and back, all the while singing, "We Shall Overcome," a song which was banned in South Africa at the time.

After Stutterheim, Biko spent almost an entire year driving around the country, visiting black student campuses, convincing students of the merits of his philosophy, which he now called "Black Consciousness."

Drawing upon the civil rights and Black Power movements in the United States, as well as anti-colonial movements in other parts of Africa, Black Consciousness was uniquely South African. Its definition of black included Africans, Indians, and coloureds, and its focus was on overcoming the psychological oppression of black people rather than resorting to an armed struggle. Biko felt that black people needed to break the oppression of their own minds; only in that way would they be able to become self-reliant.

A little more than a year later, the black caucus broke away from NUSAS to form SASO, the South African Student Organisation, a federation of black university student representative councils. Biko was elected its first president. SASO advocated replacing the term "nonwhite" with "black."

"We were being stated as nonsomething, which implied that the standard was something, and we were not that particular standard," Biko said in a later interview.

According to Biko, the NUSAS executive was at first angry and resorted to smear tactics against some of SASO's leaders in order to turn black students against them. But many in NUSAS were impressed with Biko's arguments and supported the separation.

3

A THOUSAND MILES AWAY, IN ONE of Pretoria's Union Buildings, B.J. Vorster was in his office welcoming a fellow soldier from the Ossewabrandwag.

General Hendrik Johan van den Bergh, nicknamed Tall Hendrik due to his imposing six-foot-five frame, spoke with a soft, grandfatherly voice that hid a remarkably cunning mind. A few years earlier, as minister of justice, Vorster had created South Africa's first intelligence agency and appointed van den Bergh to head it. Since then Vorster had been elected to the most powerful office in the country, and van den Bergh's star was rising with his.

But times were changing, too. Van den Bergh had just returned from a visit to the United States, where in spite of his pro-Nazi leanings, he had been welcomed with open arms. President Richard Nixon had been inaugurated earlier that year and, with Secretary of State Henry Kissinger, had embraced the "Tar Baby Option" in their relations with southern African states. The nickname was given to the policy that grew out of the Cold War, in which the United States preferred to support white regimes, even oppressive ones, over legitimate black liberation movements in Angola, Mozambique, Rhodesia, and South Africa.

Van den Bergh sat down and gave his report. He had met and spent a good portion of time with senior Central Intelligence Agency (CIA) officials, learning the inner workings of the highly regarded intelligence agency. He was inspired and wanted to create something similar for southern Africa. Vorster listened carefully, without interruption.

Finally, grim-faced, he leaned forward and explained that he had not been joking when he gave the speech at the opening ceremony of the new prison named after him. He had made it abundantly clear that he would not tolerate the breakdown of law and order in the Republic.

"So what do you propose?" he said now to van den Bergh.

Van den Bergh explained that the communist threat was real. Although they had the support of the US government, they needed to expand their own operations, to know everything that was going on, everywhere—inside the country and out.

The result of the men's discussions was the creation of the Bureau of State Security (dubbed BOSS by the press). With almost unlimited funding, the organization expanded dramatically, its tentacles spreading out to identify any threat, real or perceived, and then to assess and manage that threat. Years later, van den Bergh would gloat, "We'd never used spies, there was no need for us to use spies... We had sufficient men of our own to do all the jobs."

One of those men was Craig Williamson. At twenty-two, Williamson looked like a young Luciano Pavarotti. He had the same portly physique, a round face with ruddy apple cheeks, and a beaming smile that, years later, would shine out of a neatly trimmed beard. But on a sunny day in suburban Johannesburg, Williamson, a low-level policeman who toiled away at a boring desk job, was clean-shaven.

Two days before, he was surprised when his boss summoned him. He was introduced to two men from Special Branch, a newly formed division of the South African Police. The men were friendly and invited him to join them for a barbecue. Special Branch was known for its secrecy, and any rookie worth his salt knew not to ask any questions. The barbecue was cordial, and the men seemed genuinely interested in what he had to say.

A couple of days later, he was again picked up, but this time he was driven to an office. There a tall, stern-looking man with a chevron mustache greeted him warmly. Lieutenant Colonel Johann Coetzee was a sculptor in his spare time, an expert on communism, and head of Special Branch. He was also a protégé of van den Bergh. Although the South African Defence Force and the police did not report directly to van den Bergh's BOSS, he had maneuvered close colleagues of his—Coetzee was one of them—into key departments.

In a matter of hours, Coetzee had decided Williamson would leave his current job to enroll for a degree in political science at the University of the Witwatersrand, or Wits, as it was commonly known. Wits was the largest liberal campus in the country.

Coetzee's main aim was to have Williamson infiltrate NUSAS and report back to his handler, Piet Goosen.

Special Branch was still so caught up in Vorster's thinking of whites as the puppet masters, they had no idea Steve Biko even existed.

4

DURBAN IS A MUGGY CITY on the east coast of South Africa. It hugs the warm waters of the Indian Ocean in which, from May through July, the greatest fish migration on the planet occurs. Millions of sardines circle through the waters, attracting dolphins and seagulls, as well as hundreds of Durbanites to the beach to scoop up sardines with buckets and bare hands.

It was here, hundreds of years before, that the British Empire planted sugar cane for export to London. But the local Zulus were an unruly bunch who refused to work in the fields. The empire looked to its colony India, with its many millions of people starving and desperate for work under the tax system imposed by their colonial rulers. Thousands of indentured Indian laborers were shipped to work in Durban, leading to its distinction of having the largest population of Indians outside India.

As African, Indian, and coloured university students joined SASO in large numbers, Durban, with its spice-filled Indian bazaars, and bunny chow, a bread bowl filled with curry, became SASO's headquarters. The group of students who made up the Durban

Moment were all young, intelligent, politicized, and cosmopolitan. They spent their days smoking, debating, or going to parties where they drank cheap beer and danced to the lush voices of Miriam Makeba, Diana Ross, and Smokey Robinson.

Among them was a small group of women. Vivacious Vuyelwa Mashalaba, a striking beauty who loved giant hoop earrings and classical music, was a good friend of Biko's. She introduced a graceful and quietly confident young woman, Mamphela Ramphele, to Biko and his friends.

Biko had always been a womanizer, to the point where he and Duncan Innes, a past president of NUSAS, competed for the "Duncan Innes trophy," which was awarded to the young man who slept with the most women at a conference. And although the Immorality Act made sex across the color barrier illegal, with a sentence of seven years in prison if caught in the act, the men had no reservations about sleeping with women of all race groups.

Many women in SASO accused the men of blatant sexism. They argued the group most excluded from political discussions was black women, and such sexism only aggravated this exclusion. Other women in their circle felt that while gender, unlike race, was never high on the movement's agenda, women were encouraged to lead their own battles and not wait for the men.

In the frenetic activity around the launch of SASO, Biko and Mamphela fell in love. According to her, their relationship was a "semi-platonic friendship that frequently 'degenerated' into passion."

They spent long hours together, sharing dog-eared

banned books and listening to the speeches of Malcolm X and Martin Luther King. Biko was disorganized, and Mamphela often wrote down his thoughts as a stream of consciousness, which he later typed up with two fingers. "One has to write history to make history," he said to her.

They bonded during quiet moments as they worked on weekends at the paradoxically named Happy Valley Clinic, where they helped immunize the children of the desperately poor communities of the surrounding shantytowns.

He wrote her a love poem titled "A Love Supreme."

While she was committed to her studies but made time for activism, he was the opposite—committed to activism and occasionally making time for his studies. Biko spent much of his time writing articles for the SASO newsletter under the pseudonym Frank Talk. The articles were some of his best writing, showing his intellectual brilliance; helping to clarify his own thinking about Black Consciousness.

He often used examples from his own life to make a case. "I have lived all my conscious life in the framework of institutionalized separate development. My friendships, my love, my education, my thinking, and every other facet of my life have been carved and shaped within the context of separate development."

The contradictions of choosing the exclusiveness of Black Consciousness over the multiculturalism of NUSAS was a hot topic he addressed frequently.

He argued that blacks had to overcome two major forces of subjugation that held them back. The first was external, through the country's laws, poor pay, poor education, and the institutionalized machinery of apartheid. The second was internal, the sense of inferiority instilled in black people over centuries.

"At the heart of Black Consciousness is the realization by blacks that the most potent weapon in the hands of the oppressor is the mind of the oppressed," Biko wrote. "If one is free at heart, no man-made chains can bind one to servitude. But if one's mind is so manipulated and controlled by the oppressor then there will be nothing the oppressed can do to scare his powerful master. The first step therefore is to make the black man come to himself; to pump back life into his empty shell; to infuse him with pride and dignity; to remind him of his complicity in the crime of allowing himself to be misused and therefore letting evil reign supreme in the country of his birth."

He quoted examples of the "two-faced" attitude of black people, like his own experience with an African man who nodded and smiled even as his white boss berated him and called him an imbecile. When Biko asked him why he accepted the abuse, the man replied he had no choice because he needed the job.

Therefore, Biko saw raising pride and belief in their own strength in blacks as a vital aspect of the work of Black Consciousness. Its aim was to liberate blacks from psychological oppression and establish a new dignity in them through new attitudes and a rediscovery of their history and the culture of their people.

It was under this thinking the slogan "Black Man, You Are on Your Own" became the rallying cry for blacks all over the country.

But Biko was aware of SASO's limitations. It was a student organization with an ever-changing membership. The philosophy of Black Consciousness was in danger of dying in the realms of academia, if it did not move out into the community. He proposed a community-based cultural organization, called Black People's Convention or BPC, which would spread Black Consciousness into the wider community. Within a year of its launch, BPC had four thousand members and forty-one branches. Hardly a national movement, but not insignificant, either.

On rare occasions, Biko doubted himself. He wondered whether his focus on culture and psychology made him look like a novice to the two more established liberation organizations.

The older of these was Mandela's ANC. It was part of the Congress Alliance, which was made up of the Communist Party, the Indian Congress, and the Coloured People's Congress. The other, called the Pan Africanist Congress, or PAC, had broken away from the ANC, to form a non-racial organization where the white, Indians, and coloured minorities would fit in, with Africans leading the struggle.

Both of these older liberation organizations had resorted to armed struggle as part of their strategy, although they were determined to attack only "hard" targets like military bases and utility installations.

To Biko, Black Consciousness was addressing a different need, empowering people to think for themselves.

He was a keen proponent of Brazilian Paulo Freire's "critical pedagogy." The thrust of Freire's argument, which he makes in his book *Pedagogy of the Oppressed*, is that education should be a collaborative dialogue between students and teachers, based on the experiences of students themselves, as opposed to students being recipients of a top-down education, "banking education," in which the teacher deposits bits of knowledge—as into an empty bank account—into the minds of students.

Biko believed that, as with Freire's approach, once black people were made aware of their own entrapment as well as their own capabilities, they would be able to think for themselves and design their own liberation struggle. The other liberation organizations had a more hierarchical (banking) approach, with leaders directing people in their struggle against their oppression.

Black Consciousness's simple message to people to be proud of themselves appealed to blacks in all walks of life—artists, workers, and students. Because so many other professions were closed to them, many SASO members became teachers in black townships, where they introduced Black Consciousness to their high school students, who found its logic particularly appealing.

From a glimmer of an idea in the young Steve Biko's mind, Black Consciousness grew to become a major component of black student politics and expanded into a national political organization that, in his own words, "diminished the element of fear in the minds of black people and prepared them for leadership roles in the various facets of the black community."

5

AT THE SPRAWLING CAMPUS OF Wits in the heart of Johannesburg, Craig Williamson, who was naturally outgoing and likable, had grown a beard and thrown himself into studying political theory and international politics.

By his second year, he had successfully infiltrated the white student-activist crowd. But he couldn't hide his past in the police force; too many of his old schoolmates were at the same university and knew of it. He clung to his explanation of joining the police force only to get out of the draft, which was compulsory for all young white males, but many remained unconvinced.

He was ambitious and knew he had to overcome their doubts if he wanted to get ahead in the spying world, especially as he wasn't the only spy on campus. In fact, four of the twelve members of the university's student representative body were spies. He set about carefully planning his route onto the executive committee of NUSAS.

After the split with SASO, the organization had, under its president, Neville Curtis, become decidedly more radical. It reorganized itself into three arms: one for education, another for culture and a third,

NUSWEL, for social welfare. Jeanette Curtis, Neville's younger sister, headed NUSWEL. Jeanette was in her early twenties, a flower child of the sixties. Pretty in a girl-next-door kind of way, with thick glasses, long blonde hair, and an honest smile that revealed slightly crooked teeth. She was passionate about workers' rights and literacy.

Williamson made himself indispensable to these arms of NUSAS by volunteering for the most mundane tasks, like photocopying, which often took up enormous amounts of time. He became close friends with many executive members of NUSAS, even attending their weddings.

He was tireless in taking part in protests and was even arrested in 1972. He was released without being charged. The episode dramatically increased his credibility as an activist.

In the spring of 1973, he had another opportunity to demonstrate his commitment.

At the world's deepest gold mine, Western Deep Levels, belonging to the mining giant Anglo American, migrant workers were protesting poverty wages. For no more than a few dollars a day, close to fourteen thousand black miners took a "cage" every day down two miles into the earth, where they blasted tons of rock to bring up gold measurable only in ounces. In early September, police opened fire on the protesting miners, killing twelve and wounding thirty-eight others.

Williamson, along with other NUSAS members, organized a protest march to Anglo American's headquarters in downtown Johannesburg. The students gathered outside the glass doors, and when Anglo security tried to close the doors on them,

Williamson used his large body to ram his way into the lobby. He was arrested and charged with riotous assembly, a charge that was subsequently dropped, but the escapade helped convince his fellow students of his activist commitment.

He was soon elected treasurer of NUSAS.

6

THE POLICE VANS CAME IN the early morning, a few hours past midnight. The cops banged on the doors of the houses or apartments, yelling in Afrikaans, tactics that were meant to scare the residents from their sleep. They dragged their targets out of bed, ordered them to dress, and shoved them into the back of the van.

The success of SASO and BPC under the philosophy of Black Consciousness inevitably brought the unwelcome attention of Vorster's government. Almost all the top leaders of the two organizations were at one point or another detained for questioning under the sweeping powers of the Terrorism Act.

Except for Steve Biko. Instead, they shackled him with a banning order.

Banning orders were a unique form of house arrest. Under a five - and sometimes ten-year banning order, you were confined to your house and your place of work. You were not allowed to be near workers, students, or a court of law where you could organize protests. You were not allowed to publish anything that might "harm the state," or to provide education to anyone other than your own child. For some banned people, only a medical doctor or your closest family members, whose names were clearly listed on the banning order itself, were allowed to visit you. All this was monitored by twenty-four-hour police surveillance.

In Biko's case, the state banned him to his hometown of Ginsberg, near King William's Town in the Eastern Cape. The local police were assigned to monitor him.

Soon, the security police chief of the region would be Colonel Piet Goosen, none other than Williamson's handler.

In 1973, in the Eastern Cape, Biko set about regaining the freedom his ancestors, the Xhosas, had lost.

In this harsh landscape, for the hundred years between 1779 and 1879, in what have come to be known as the Cape Frontier Wars, the Xhosas, resisted British settlers' attempts to steal their land and their cattle and destroy their way of life. During the sixth of nine wars, in 1835, King Hintsa of the Xhosa nation was killed, his body dismembered by British troops. His head was never found and was presumed to be taken to Britain as a trophy.

Biko thought often of Mamphela. He missed her. Their relationship had followed a tortuous path. On a visit back to her hometown she had reconnected with her old boyfriend. He had proposed to her, and they were married soon after.

Disappointed, Biko threw himself into launching BPC. And then he met a cousin of his friend Vuyelwa. Ntsiki Mashalaba, a nurse who was quiet and full of inner poise, laughingly accepted his meager gifts of bars of chocolate. She tolerated his hectic schedule and often agreed to meet him at odd places like the railway station as he dashed from one meeting to another. They were married in his hometown of Ginsberg, followed by a small celebration at mamCethe's (his mother) house. In 1971, Ntsiki gave him her greatest gift, their son, Nkosinathi.

For many people, becoming a parent leads them to confront their own mortality for the first time. Holding in one's arms a fragile life that is entirely dependent on one is often a life-altering event. Biko was no different. Later he voiced his thoughts on his own death.

"The bond between life and death is absolute. You are either alive and proud, or you are dead, and when you are dead, you can't care anyway. And your method of death can itself be a politicizing thing."

Banned to Ginsberg, he moved, with his wife and son, into mamCethe's house. The home was a hive of activity. His siblings lived there as well, and friends were always welcome. The community had strong bonds and received the young family with open arms.

But the police were always watching. The relationship between them and Biko was obscenely personal but one-sided. They knew his family and often referred to them by their first names. As soon as a visitor arrived, they would be knocking on the door, demanding to know their names and the purpose of their visit. More often than not, as the police walked up to the door, the children signaled their arrival, and the visitor would quickly exit Biko's room and start chatting with one of the other family members.

Life in rural Ginsberg was a far cry from vibrant

Durban. The police hoped the isolation would break not only Biko's influence but also his spirit.

But he was unshakable. Unable to continue his medical studies, he enrolled for a correspondence law degree. His larger-than-life presence drew a lively group of activists to the area. In a whitewashed Anglican Church on Leopold Street in the heart of the town, the small group of activists ran projects that created home industries and jobs, an educational fund, and day care. They set up programs that provided leadership training. They worked at instilling values of self-reliance and self-help in their community.

Soon, "white" King William's Town began to hear of him. Donald Woods, a liberal editor of East London's *Daily Dispatch,* wrote multiple editorials accusing SASO of racism because it excluded whites. Biko invited Woods to meet with him. They met in the small weed-choked backyard of the church.

Later Woods wrote, "My first impression was of his size... He stood at least a couple of inches over me, and had the bulky build of a heavyweight boxer... He greeted me with reserve."

Woods blurted out that he didn't have to "bloody well" apologize for being born white or for racial policies he didn't support. Biko listened carefully and then broke out into a huge, toothy grin. "I don't reject liberalism or white liberals as such. I reject only the concept that black liberation can be achieved through the leadership of white liberals," he said.

They spoke for hours, with Woods eventually agreeing to let Biko's colleague, Mapetla Mohapi, write a Black Consciousness column for the *Daily Dispatch.*

Politically, Biko stuck steadfastly to a non-violent position. His point of view was pragmatic. He knew any suggestions of a violent struggle or communism would scare the authorities into banning the Black Consciousness movement.

He also found time to party and dance. One of his favorite songs was Donny Hathaway's "To Be Young, Gifted and Black," and his favorite Xhosa composer was Tyamzashe. Biko drank and danced at the local *shebeens* (taverns), where a group of youths known as the Cubans were happy to protect him from the police. A family friend, Xolile Mangcu, describes an incident where "Bra Steve" was having a drink at a local tavern when the police surrounded the place. The Cubans gathered together and hastily organized a fake wedding between two of their friends, and in the celebrations Biko escaped to a neighbor's house, dove in through a window, and fell asleep on the bed while waiting for the coast to clear.

But one source of antagonism all round was Biko's relationship with Mamphela. By now Mamphela had graduated as a medical doctor, but her marriage had disintegrated. She and Biko began a long-distance affair. Then she transferred to a local hospital to complete her medical internship, and a few months later she moved closer to Ginsberg.

With a donation from a sympathetic German donor, she started Zanempilo Clinic. Under a small staff, the clinic grew into an exceptional facility, providing outpatient care, maternity care, and a mobile clinic for its community. It provided critical services in a country where there was only one doctor for every forty thousand black patients compared to one for every six hundred white patients. It was also a great cover for political activities and a place where Biko could meet with visitors without being detected by the police. He would steal out in the dark of the night from his mother's house to attend meetings at the clinic.

But he also often spent the night with Mamphela. Their love affair was now out in the open, causing a rift between Ntsiki and him.

Many in the Black Consciousness movement were also concerned of the example he was setting as a national leader, especially to impressionable young people. Robert Sobukwe, leader of the PAC, voiced his concerns to Aelred Stubbs, Biko's priest and confidant. Stubbs discussed the matter with Biko, who responded angrily that Sobukwe was out of date. Later he wrote to Stubbs and this time claimed he had a right to privacy.

Finally he wrote again to Stubbs, "I've been reflecting on my letters to you... and cannot help feeling I have been unkind to you." He went on to explain how difficult life was, even though he had a loving and supportive family, "which is fully committed to my commitment, if not to the cause itself."

In spite of the friction, Biko continued his affair with Mamphela. In late 1973, she became pregnant. It was a difficult pregnancy and when she had a medical emergency during which she thought she had almost lost the baby, Mamphela opted to rest at her mother's house, a twelve-hour drive away from Ginsberg.

She gave birth to their baby girl, Lerato, meaning "love" in Sotho. Two and a half months later, the little girl succumbed to a bout of severe pneumonia, having never been held by her father who, due to his banning order, was not allowed to travel to see her.

7

ON MONDAY, MAY 3, 1976, twelve years after Mandela's statement from the dock at Pretoria's Supreme Court, Steve Biko took the stand in the same court. He sauntered to the witness stand, sat down after being sworn in, and leveled his steady gaze on the crowd gathered in the courtroom. The case was broadcast on radio and covered extensively in the press.

David Soggot, a human-rights lawyer for the defense, stood up to begin his questioning. "Mr. Biko, I think we should first go through the essential elements of your personal history. You were born in 1946 in King William's Town, is that correct?"

And so began five days of the most astonishing public testimony by Biko.

He was not on trial. But nine of his fellow SASO leaders were. They had organized rallies to celebrate Mozambique's independence from Portugal. Biko had been uneasy about the rallies. He worried about the risk of arrests and banning of the organization for an event that had little possibility of significant gain for the movement. But the organizers went ahead with the rallies, and the government, in a national operation, detained two hundred SASO activists. The "SASO Nine" were charged with inciting racial hatred under the Terrorism Act. When asked to testify on their behalf, Biko said, "These are our folks... For as long as they are in the hands of the enemy we should get them out."

Through careful questioning, Soggot used the courtroom to put Black Consciousness on trial. In doing so, he gave Biko a public platform from which to defend it. He allowed Biko ample time to not only define his philosophy and its growth from an idea into a movement, but also expand on a range of subjects, like the definition of black, and his thinking on democracy, education, and disinvestments.

"Were there any discussions that dealt with the future of the whites?" Soggot asked.

"We were not discussing the future of whites per se, but the future of our society," Biko replied.

The judge then intervened, "Can it not be said that you are trying to achieve your end in such a way that you are building up a hostile power bloc?"

Unflappable as always, Biko replied, "On the contrary. What I say is that our methods give hope. Black people don't have any hope, they don't see a way ahead. They are defeated persons who live with their misery."

At the end of the trial, in spite of Biko's efforts, the SASO Nine were convicted and sentenced to between five and ten years on Robben Island. But Biko's testimony had been heard far and wide in the country.

Fifty miles away in Soweto, an overpopulated African-only township south of Johannesburg, a scrawny young man with mutton-chop sideburns and a fondness for fashionable clothes, was riveted by Biko's testimony. Nineteen-year-old Teboho MacDonald Mashinini, known to everyone as Tsietsi, was the second son in a family of eleven boys and two girls.

He was energetic, extrovert and a gifted athlete who excelled at karate. His mother, Nomkhitha, whose own ambitions to become a nurse had been thwarted, showered her children with books. As a result, Tsietsi became a voracious reader and a formidable debater. His friends called him Shakespeare's friend in Africa.

He was also a natural leader. As a young boy he enrolled two of his brothers and four friends into a society he called the Secret Seven, based on the books by the children's author Enid Blyton.

During his freshman year at Morris Isaacson School, Tsietsi's history teacher was Abraham Tiro, a SASO member. A few years before, Tiro had given a speech at his university in which he excoriated the government's inferior Bantu education system, which was designed to educate Africans for a life of unskilled labor. Angered by the speech, the university expelled him, an act that resulted in black university students throughout the country going on boycott in support of Tiro's reinstatement.

In 1974, the students got news that Tiro had been killed by a letter bomb in Botswana. They had no doubt it was the work of Vorster's government, and years later Gordon Winter, a journalist and an informer, indeed fingered van den Bergh's BOSS in the attack.

With teachers like Tiro, the students at Morris Isaacson became highly politically aware. They expanded their political education by exchanging banned books, covered in brown paper, in the bathroom stalls.

Tsietsi's older brother, Rocks, after his initial introduction to Black Consciousness, came to believe an armed struggle was critical to ending apartheid. He joined the ANC.

Tsietsi, on the other hand, mesmerized the crowd at the launch of the local chapter of the South African Student Movement (SASM), the high school sister organization of SASO, and was elected president.

The two brothers often argued over the merits of the strategies of their respective organizations. Tsietsi's branch of SASM held monthly meetings that focused on cultural events, poetry reading, and discussion of African literature. They often invited a Black Consciousness leader to speak at their meetings.

As the midyear examinations approached, Nomkhitha began to pressure her children to study. But Mpho and Dee, her fourth - and fifth-born sons, were depressed. They were in middle school, and the government had decided to enforce its rule that half the subjects, especially geography, history and mathematics, in African middle schools be taught in Afrikaans.

African students in South Africa hated Afrikaans. Derived from Dutch and German, Afrikaans was the language spoken by prison wardens and white policemen when they stopped or arrested an African for not having his or her much-hated *dompas* (compulsory ID document). It was also the language spoken by the white bosses deep in the gold mines, and it was the language spoken in parliament, which excluded blacks.

The middle school midyear exam papers were to be in Afrikaans. The issue had been simmering for a few years, but the Department of Bantu Administration had usually allowed schools to opt out of the requirement.

But in January 1976, Vorster appointed Andries Treurnicht as deputy minister in charge of Bantu education. Treurnicht was an evangelical white supremacist who had been chairman of the Broederbond two years before. He was determined to put blacks in their place.

Tsietsi knew the Afrikaans decree would soon be applied to high schools as well. As his brothers struggled with words like *verhouding* for proportion, *vermenigvuldiging* for multiplication, and *riviermond* for estuary, and as teachers who could barely speak Afrikaans themselves relied on dictionaries to help them, Tsietsi and his fellow SASM members held a meeting to discuss the issue.

Within a week of the meeting, Tsietsi Mashinini would become the most wanted man in South Africa.

8

IT WAS A SUNDAY, JUNE 13, 1976. The day outside was gray and cold. Inside the community center, Tsietsi stood up to speak. "We have sent petitions to the inspector of schools. We have been ignored. We have requested a meeting with him. Our requests have been ignored. So now we say this is enough!"

The five-hundred-strong crowd of students was restless and militant. They broke out into song, and some of the youngsters began a gumboot dance. The energetic dance originated in the gold mines and is thought to have been a way of secret communications to avoid the scrutiny of white bosses.

Tsietsi continued, "We, the black students in South Africa, are being fed the type of education that will domesticate us to become better tools for the white man."

He then went on to use his oratory skills to woo and cajole his colleagues into agreeing to a student march on Wednesday, June 16, the first day of the midyear exams. With passion he quoted Tennyson's "The Charge of the Light Brigade," written in honor of soldiers in the Crimean War.

When can their glory fade?
O the wild charge they made!
All the world wondered.
Honour the charge they made,
Honour the Light Brigade,
Noble six hundred.

After some debate, where those who said the march idea was foolish or downright dangerous were outvoted, Tsietsi was elected to head the committee that would lead the protests. Over the next two days, the committee members spread out into Soweto. They canvassed students, convincing them to take part in the march. They made it clear that parents were not to be told of the event, and above all, they warned students to be disciplined—no violence, just a one-day march.

On June 15, the day before the march, Tsietsi, with a fellow student, walked into the principal's office. "Sir, we'd like to report that tomorrow we will be marching. Do you think it's a wise idea?"

The principal, Lekgau Mathabathe, said, "Well, boys, if you think the grass is dry and the winds are blowing in the right direction, go and bend the grass."

In a festive atmosphere, hundreds of students spent the afternoon secretly making placards and banners that read "Away with Afrikaans" and "Down with Bantu Education."

On the morning of Wednesday, June 16, a blustery winter's day with the smell of coal-fires in the air, Tsietsi and his fellow committee members met early at their school to review their plans. Slowly the rest of the school gathered in the schoolyard for the Lord's Prayer. Everyone was whispering and restless; the excitement ran through the crowd like electricity. The plan was for each school to march to Orlando Stadium where they would sing "Nkosi Sikelel' iAfrika" (God Bless Africa), the unofficial anthem of black people in South Africa.

Then they would disperse. The most important thing, Tsietsi reminded everyone, was to avoid provoking the police.

At the back of the crowd, the seniors unfurled a banner. Tsietsi shouted, "Let's march."

The crowd snaked out of the gates. The leaders in front shouted, "Amandla!" Power! The reply echoed back from a hundred voices: "Ngawethu!" To us! The younger kids farther back, many of them in middle grades, sang freedom songs and held hands. The girls in their shiny black shoes, white ankle socks, and teeny uniform dresses, and the boys in their gray trousers and white shirts, looked cute and like they were ready for a field trip.

Like a river with many tributaries, students from other schools merged into the growing flood. By the time they reached Orlando West, the protest had swelled to an estimated twenty thousand.

"Students of Soweto! Today, today we say no more! No more Afrikaans! No to oppression! Do we say no more?"

Thousands roared their approval and replied, "No more! No to Afrikaans!"

It was like any of the weekend soccer matches played out on the dusty fields of Soweto.

Tsietsi and his friends linked arms and held the front line as the crowd behind followed. The sturdy voices of the children rose in song and hymn into the crisp air. As students from different schools joined one another, the river of young people became an unstoppable flood.

But stop the flood was exactly what Colonel Kleingeld and his riot squad of fifty policemen set out to do. They trundled their Hippos, armored vehicles mounted with twin machine guns, across the road to bar the way.

Tsietsi tried to approach the riot police to speak with them, but the officers ignored him. The colonel ordered police dogs to be unleashed. As the terrified students screamed and scattered, he commanded his men to fire tear gas into the crowd.

The students had never experienced tear gas before. Blinded by the stinging gas, to the children the sound of the canisters mimicked the sound of bullets. They panicked.

Writhing in pain, some students pelted their attackers with stones. Some threw the searing tear-gas canisters back at the police. Colonel Kleingeld fired the first shot, and although accounts vary, within minutes two students had suffered fatal bullet wounds: thirteen-year-old Hector Pieterson and seventeen-year-old Hastings Ndhlovu. The autopsy later performed on Hector suggested he was bending down, most probably running away, when he was shot in the back. The bullet mutilated his right kidney, barreled its way through his body, and exited through the left carotid artery in his neck.

Witnessing the chaos, Tsietsi climbed onto an old

bulldozer and pleaded hoarsely with the crowd to disperse. But it was too late.

As enraged students ran through the township, some setting fire to cars and government-owned liquor stores that they viewed as symbols of government authority, helicopters located and tear-gassed from above anyone in a school uniform. Riot police went door to door and dragged out students, randomly shooting at anyone running away from them. Eight-year-old Lilly Mithi was killed by a bullet that entered her back and shattered her heart as she stopped to help her aunt. Twelve-year-old Hermina Leroke was shot through the heart. Amos Mokoena, described as "youth" in the postmortem report, was shot twice, killed by a bullet that went through his lung.

Tsietsi's brother Mpho, took refuge in a house with a frightened group of students. The owner kept a lookout and hours later when the coast was clear, Mpho set out for home.

Dee, Tsietsi's other brother, overwhelmed by the tear gas and ensuing chaos was frozen to the spot when he saw a young boy who was shot in the leg trying to hobble away. Finally, he ran to a nearby house, where he tried to hide in an outside toilet, only to find it already filled with terrified students. Unable to stop themselves from coughing, the students stumbled out. Two women in a nearby house took them in. They washed the tear gas out of their eyes, and Dee finally made it home late in the evening.

As darkness fell, over fifty students had been killed and almost seven hundred injured. Two white men, Melville Edelstein, a sociologist, and J.

H. B. Esterhuizen, an inspector, were killed during the rioting.

Roadblocks sealed off Soweto, and paramilitary reinforcements were rushed in to crush the uprising. In the eyes of law enforcement, the children were criminals, and they did not hesitate to use live ammunition.

Baragwanath Hospital in Soweto and its satellite clinics were swamped with schoolchildren, most shot above the waist, and many dead on arrival. Police followed students into the hospital, seeking to arrest those they thought were leaders of the protests. Appalled, doctors refused to comply. Police tried to force clerks to hand over the admission notes. The clerks banded together with doctors and agreed to document shot students as having "abscesses," and the doctors admitted the patients to the surgical ward for "drainage of abscesses."

Thousands of children slept under bridges and in the homes of strangers, too terrified to return home. Smoke from burning buildings and vehicles rose up into the night sky and choked the township. The rest of the world woke up to the brutality of the South African regime when Sam Nzima's iconic image of the limp body of Hector, covered in blood, being carried by Mbuyisa Makhubu, with Hector's distraught sister Antoinette running alongside, was splashed across the front pages of global newspapers.

Tsietsi tried to help as many students as he could. Finally, around midnight, he made his way to the home of Drake Koka, a trade unionist and leader in the Black Consciousness movement.

I was a senior at a high school in an Indians-only suburb near Johannesburg when the shooting began.

My family hoped I would become a doctor. My mom had been shipped off to India as a teenager, where she spent her days waking up before dawn to milk cows. She was never allowed to attend school. She was in her late teens when she returned to South Africa, only to have her marriage arranged almost as soon as her ship docked. She had a feminist mind-set and high expectations for me to go to college. My dad, a struggling lawyer and a self-confessed nerd who knew Nelson Mandela and Oliver Tambo well because their law practice was in the same building as his, ignited my love for reading by buying me comics every weekend.

But getting admission into the one black medical school in the country would be quite difficult. Two of the other six were English-speaking and liberal enough to accept up to twenty black students per year, provided the minister of education himself granted them permission. The rest were for whites only.

On June 16, although we had no cell phones or social media, we heard of the shooting in under an hour. We, the prefects of the school, gathered in the dust of our sports field and decided to go on a school boycott.

We were not alone. As the news spread, black students spilled into the streets, determined to overthrow the "system." The tinder that was South Africa under apartheid had been ignited. In the ensuing months, students all over the country joined the school boycott.

Many Indian and coloured students, although unaffected by the Afrikaans decree, nevertheless felt they were very much part of the struggle against apartheid. Every day we arrived at school dressed in our uniforms and gathered in the sports field to sing freedom songs. Our teachers were largely sympathetic. When the police patrolled by, we booed and jeered at them. Occasionally they baton-charged us, but there were no shootings.

The weeks dragged on. The students became bored and restless. There were moments when I, too, wished we could go back to class, but given what was happening in the rest of the country, I knew we had little choice. Five weeks later, by the time we called off the boycott, rumors were swirling that three girls in our school were pregnant.

We had less than three months left to the final examinations. Our math teacher, determined to whip us into shape, acquired the white schools' final exam paper. Close to three-quarters of our class got an A. When we took our own Indian exam paper, only a quarter of us scored As. That was when I realized how easy the white school papers were. The African students took the JMB exams, and I knew how difficult those were.

It seems obvious in hindsight, but years later, in university, I learned that most of my white professors who sat on the university admissions committee had no idea the high school exam papers were so skewed to advantage white students.

It was clear proof of how the apartheid government perpetuated the myth of white intellectual superiority and black inferiority.

9

TSIETSI SPENT THE DAYS AFTER June 16 maneuvering through Soweto. The township resembled a war zone. Smoldering vehicles and debris—much of it school shoes and uniforms—littered the streets, which smelled of burning tires.

Through arrests and interrogations of students, some so young that a few threats against their families was enough to convince them to cave, the police pieced together Tsietsi's pivotal role in the march. They then began regular raids of his home.

The first time, they arrived at two in the morning. They surrounded the home with their Hippos, and a swarm of armed men stormed the house. Their pounding on the door terrified Tsietsi's dazed family. The policemen screamed in Afrikaans and rampaged through the home, searching and dismantling bookshelves for banned materials. Nomkhitha, Tsietsi's mother, clutched her babies—the youngest were the girls, twins and still toddlers—and watched with grim determination. The raids became a nightly event, and often the children startled at the slightest sound. Sometimes the family would even be waiting when the Hippos pulled up. Nomkhitha cursed the police in Xhosa and English, and they often swore back at the *"kaffir"* (racial slur for African) bitch in Afrikaans. Tsietsi's father, Joseph, spent most of his time trying to prevent the multilingual cursing match from deteriorating into Nomkhitha's arrest.

Tsietsi and his committee regrouped. They enrolled more members. They tried to get students to return to school. At the same time, they worked with the hastily formed Black Parents Committee and the workers unions to plan a national work boycott and a march on August 4. The plan was to march into Johannesburg and demand the release of detained students.

The activists held secret midnight meetings with a sympathetic man who ran a printing press in downtown Johannesburg. He printed thousands of leaflets for them.

On the morning of August 4 Tsietsi's fellow students spread out onto the platforms of railway stations throughout Soweto and raised banners that said "Azikhwelwa!" We won't ride! The protest, and the slogan, originated from twenty years before when Nelson Mandela's ANC, together with the South African Indian Congress, organized the Defiance Campaign, one of the largest non-violent passive-resistance campaigns in the tradition of Mahatma Gandhi, who had spent twenty years in South Africa mobilizing Indians against the British government before his return to India.

Tsietsi himself led the school march from Morris Isaacson School. Riot police lined up their Hippos to prevent the march.

Apartheid's founding fathers had planned for such an occurrence by ensuring only a single road led into and out of any black housing area. The police blocked the road and fired tear gas. As the noxious fumes billowed out over the crowd, the students again retaliated with stones. They scattered and regrouped to attack the homes of black policemen and suspected collaborators and spies.

Soweto was again on fire. This time the police announced a reward, equivalent to a year's salary for some, for information leading to Tsietsi's capture. He was now a hunted man.

For weeks following June 16, distraught parents still searched morgues for their missing children. The morgues were a horrific sight, filled with hundreds of bodies, almost all children, with numbers pasted on their foreheads and piled one on top of the other.

Others worried about where their children were sleeping or eating, and yet others begged the police to provide information on whether their kids had been arrested.

Students themselves refused to return to school. They marched through townships, setting fire to symbols of apartheid, such as the distinctive green government-owned Putco buses and liquor stores run by the state, hated as another means of oppression of black people. Police stations and Bantu Administration offices, where the loathsome administration work of apartheid—like fingerprinting to control the movement of Africans—was conducted, were firebombed. Some suspected police collaborators were murdered and their cars torched.

The Afrikaner newspapers blared their headlines:

The Transvaler "Shock Violence, Whites Chopped to Death" and the *Beeld* "Hell in Soweto," with a photo of a sea of students, throwing flaming bottles at a group of policemen armed with rifles.

The stark picture of the bleeding Hector Pieterson being carried away made the world sit up and take notice. The Nordic countries recommended a weapons embargo against South Africa. Within days of June 16, the UN Security Council convened an urgent meeting at the request of the African states and issued a unanimous condemnation of South Africa.

Over a matter of a few weeks, hundreds of students were killed, thousands injured, and thousands more arrested. A countrywide state of emergency was declared, and the army became a regular presence in black areas.

But the government's allies were steadfast.

When Vorster met with Henry Kissinger, the USA Secretary of State, in West Germany, a week after June 16, the agenda did not touch upon the shooting of hundreds of black children in the townships. Instead the two cracked locker-room jokes and plotted a change of government in Rhodesia with Kissinger saying, "I can handle Congress. I'll just not tell them very much."

PART 2

10

HOUNDED BY THE POLICE AND the army, an estimated four thousand young men and women, mainly black, went into exile during the unrest that became known as the Soweto Uprising. They left by car or by train. Some shaved their heads and changed their clothes in a vain attempt to disguise themselves, although more often than not their youth and their complexions gave them away.

Years later, students narrated disturbing stories of arrest and torture by the security police. A fifteen-year-old boy described being held in solitary confinement for six months. Policemen came in periodically to beat him and urinate on him. Eventually he was released without being charged.

The youngsters left behind their girlfriends, boyfriends, parents, brothers, and sisters. Some just wanted an education; others, hardened by their treatment at the hands of the police, were determined to fight for their freedom by joining Umkhonto, the armed wing of Mandela's ANC.

But Umkhonto leaders were caught by surprise by the student exodus. They herded many of the youngsters into refugee camps in Mozambique and Botswana where they made some attempt to identify them. This was almost impossible, as most of the youth had escaped with no identity documents, clothing, or money. The youngsters spent many months, and sometimes more than a year, in the camps, together with refugees from Mozambique and Angola where the USSR and the USA were conducting proxy wars as part of their Cold War strategy.

The group of youngsters who joined Umkhonto and trained as soldiers were dubbed the "June 16 detachment." They were the most critical turning point in the history of the fight against apartheid. Their large numbers swell the ranks of Umkhonto and gave the ANC a new urgency and legitimacy in the eyes of the world's nations. Many of the youth trained in guerrilla warfare and returned to their country of birth to become thorns in the side of the apartheid government for the next two decades.

One out of every five youngsters escaping the country was a young woman. Oliver Tambo called them the "flowers of the revolution." Barely adults, many of the women became dedicated soldiers.

The exodus of so many young people didn't happen overnight, especially as the borders of the country were heavily guarded. They needed help. An underground freedom train. There were many people, of all race groups, who helped the students evade police and eventually escape the country. But they were overwhelmed with the sheer number of students wanting to leave.

That's where Craig Williamson entered the picture.

For Williamson, the events of June 16 were a perfect opportunity to advance his spy career. He helped numerous students cross the border into Botswana, no doubt delivering them straight into the hands of the security police. He was well known as the man to speak to if one needed to escape. Ironically, most people reported his route to be the safest way to get out.

It was not only black students escaping the violence in the townships who sought Williamson's help, but also many white students who were being increasingly harassed and restricted.

Three months after June 16, Jeanette Curtis was arrested under Section 6 of the Terrorism Act, a section that allowed for indefinite detention. She was interrogated and kept in solitary confinement for two months.

In November, upon her release, she was banned for five years. A few months later, she met and fell in love with Marius Schoon, a white political activist and teacher. Marius was a tall man with a large beard and a baritone voice. He had been recently released after serving twelve years in prison for a failed bomb attack on a Johannesburg police station. Marius was immediately banned upon his release. As two banned people, Jeanette and Marius could not legally meet, go on a date or to the movies, or even be seen having coffee together. But the upheaval in the country drew them together even more. A year after June 16, Jeanette and Marius escaped the country into Botswana.

The previous year, after a trip to Europe in his capacity as NUSAS treasurer, Williamson had already submitted to his handlers a detailed plan to infiltrate the ANC.

After the events of June 16, with the flight of so many students, van den Bergh knew most of the youngsters were leaving to join the ANC and its Communist Party ally. To Williamson's delight, he gave his approval for Williamson to put his plan into action.

In late 1976, Williamson was assigned two bosses. He still reported directly via his handler Piet Goosen, to Johan Coetzee in the Special Branch section of the police, but for his plan on infiltrating the ANC, he was assigned to BOSS.

11

THE MASHININI FAMILY GATHERED IN their small "matchbox" house. The young boys were excited that Tsietsi was home, and the two youngest, Linda and Lindi, competed for his attention. He adored them and was quite happy to change their diapers when necessary.

The family formed a circle and held hands. Joseph, a guild member of the Methodist Church, said a prayer. For the first time in weeks all his children, except his eldest, Rocks, were at home. Rocks's ambitions to become an engineer had been derailed by the unrest. He had gone underground and joined Umkhonto.

For weeks, Tsietsi, flushed with adrenaline and convinced of his own invincibility had been playing an elaborate cat-and-mouse game with the police. Nomkhitha heard stories of him appearing with a basket of fruit at the bedside of a girl paralyzed after being shot by the police, escaping from a political meeting dressed as a girl, and being caught on camera cheekily throwing the black power salute from a car right in front of a police station. Both the police and the residents of Soweto, now nicknamed him the Scarlet Pimpernel, a fictional character who rescued aristocrats from the guillotine during the French Revolution. Articulate and passionate, Tsietsi became the voice of the students on worldwide television when he secretly gave an interview to journalists from Thames TV in London.

Tsietsi had come home a few times, often while his mother was at work. He had sneaked in through the back door, changed his clothes, grabbed some food, and disappeared again.

Now he hugged his mother tightly, and she kissed him on the cheek. His father, always so severe that Tsietsi and Rocks had nicknamed him "the Sheriff," hugged him for a long time, finally releasing him and whispering good-bye.

Tsietsi left, not knowing when he would see his family again.

12

IT WAS EARLY 1977. THE country was slowly calming down. Craig Williamson, together with his colleagues in Special Branch, devised a pantomime.

The police raided his apartment and seized his passport. He planned his "escape" with a fellow student who had undergone a terrifying ordeal at the hands of the police and been banned for five years.

Under assumed names, Williamson and his fellow student drove the almost five-hour journey to the South African-Botswana border. They waited until dark and then set off to walk the last ten miles through countryside that was more home to puff adders and spitting cobras than to humans. At sunrise the two men crawled over the barbed-wire fence separating the countries.

In Botswana, Williamson set out to look for a job. He contacted Lars-Gunnar Eriksson, head of the International University Exchange Fund (IUEF), a Scandinavian aid agency that had provided funds to help people escape the country. Williamson had met Eriksson on his previous trip to Europe, and the two had become friends.

But Williamson also had reason to be anxious. His career in international espionage would come to an abrupt end if Eriksson got wind of his past in the police force.

Indeed, when the South African Council of Churches learned that IUEF was hiring Williamson, they warned them of their suspicions that Williamson was a spy. But Eriksson ignored the warnings, in part because as an independent aid agency he wanted to set IUEF apart from the Swedish government, which had aligned itself firmly with the ANC, and in part because he liked Williamson.

To his relief, Williamson soon found himself in Geneva, filing reports for the IUEF.

It was mid-1977 and in Geneva's Old Town, spring came to an end. As the hot days of summer replaced the cooler days, red geraniums peeked out from window boxes on the streets around Saint Pierre's Cathedral. The sun glinted off the stained-glass windows of the cathedral, with its eclectic mix of Roman and Gothic architecture. The city came to life as tourists in sundresses and shorts ambled through alleys lined with cobblestones, corner bistros, art galleries, and antique shops.

Williamson, with his Danish-South African wife, Ingrid, made a home in this idyllic city. With his double salary, one from the IUEF and the other from his spy work for Special Branch, he could afford a more than comfortable living. He loved sushi, eating often at a restaurant called Kyoto.

He was placed in charge of providing funding for people who needed to get out of South Africa. At the same time he sent reports through his wife back to Piet Goosen.

Around the first anniversary of June 16, Williamson received a request that aroused his curiosity. He was asked to fund Steve Biko's travels.

Williamson knew the request was bad news, and he informed Piet Goosen, his handler.

13

WHILE WILLIAMSON WAS SETTLING DOWN in Geneva, I was in my second year at medical school, at Williamson's alma mater, Wits. There were two hundred of us clustered in groups of four, around tables in the dissection hall. The students were all white except for one African, two coloureds and us seven Indians. In front of us lay more than fifty bodies, carefully preserved in gallons of formaldehyde, phenol, methanol, and glycerin.

I felt a little giddy from the sweet, antiseptic smell of embalming fluid. It was a solemn occasion. In front of the class the head of Anatomy, world-renowned palaeoanthropologist, Professor Tobias, stood with a chaplain, a Hindu priest, an imam and a rabbi. They each blessed the bodies and led us through short prayers. The service ended with Prof requesting us to respect the bodies in front of us.

Ours was a John Doe. An African man, more than six feet tall, immensely muscular with a square jaw and smudges of gray at the temples, and judging by his physique he must have been a miner. He was so large it took all four of us to turn him over when we came to dissect the muscles on his back.

Over the course of a year, John taught me more than any textbook or lecturer. It was John who taught me the intricacies of the brachial plexus in his armpit, the course of the vagus nerve all the way from his brain down to his diaphragm and the three gorgeous heads of the deltoid muscle of his shoulder.

Sometimes, though not often enough, I wondered about his family. Who were they? Did he have a wife, children, and grandchildren maybe? They would surely be horrified to know that I was dissecting his body. Learning from it. Maybe they knew he was dead, but couldn't afford to bury him?

Over time I came to realize mining was the single most important driving force behind the creation of apartheid. The mining industry began more than a hundred years before, in 1860, when Erasmus Jacobs, the young son of a white farmer, while fishing in the Orange River spied a piece of stone the size of a tiny egg. It was grimy but glistened when held to the light. He had the stone for a month before his neighbor admired it and offered to buy it. Mrs. Jacobs, Erasmus's mother, laughed and refused any payment. She gave the stone to the neighbor as a gift. The stone turned out to be the 21 Carat Eureka Diamond, the first diamond found in South Africa, and it heralded the start of the diamond rush.

Some of the fields were alluvial fields where diamonds were found in loose soil and not cemented into solid rock. The "natives" were an abundant supply of cheap labor, and were quickly put to use. Lines and lines of African people, on their hands and knees, gravel digging deep into their skin, crawling on the ground picking up diamonds and plopping them into tin cans around their necks.

For miners like our John Doe life was just as harsh as his ancestors a century before. Imagine going more than two miles, the distance say between the Upper East Side to Times Square in New York City, straight into the muggy, stuffy bowels of the Earth. Now imagine doing this packed into a metal cage with twenty other people, three or four cages stacked one on top of each other. As you perspire you also sense the pressure of the rock around you. For every mile you travel beneath the surface, the temperature rises 15° F, and the pressure increases at a rate of thousands of pounds-force per square inch. The rock often talks, occasionally spits slivers out at you, usually just before a major rock fall.

In the world's deepest mines in South Africa, for more than a century, hundreds of thousands of miners have been descending down into the Earth every day to bring up gold measured in mere ounces.

And it's not only gold and diamonds they dig for. Even today, South Africa is the world's fifth-largest mining country with wealth in coal and minerals like chrome, manganese, platinum, vanadium, palladium and zirconium and a number of other unpronounceable "iums" estimated to be in the trillions of dollars.

Families like John's had their ancestral land confiscated and could no longer live off their farms. The men were forced to leave their families in rural areas to seek work on the mines, which swallowed them up at an alarming rate. They were housed in crowded, single-sex hostels, not allowed visits from their families and given leave to go home only for

Easter and Christmas. South Africa's migrant labor system was unique in that the miners were not allowed to settle with their families near their place of employment. Prostitution and sexually transmitted diseases were rampant.

The widows of white miners were entitled to a decent lifelong pension, but there was no pension for black widows, only a one-off maximum grant that was half of what a white widow received in a year for her life.

Often, like our John Doe, the wives of most African miners never knew their husbands had died, swallowed up by South Africa's gold and diamond machinery.

14

THE SINGLE NAKED LIGHT BULB above him buzzed periodically. The cold from the concrete floor spread like tentacles through his body. The walls were a dull gray, and his single blanket, a similar gray, smelled of stale sweat.

But it mattered little to Steve Biko. It was his third time in prison.

What pained him the most was the arrest of the people around him. Mamphela was arrested together with almost all the staff at the clinic. Her fourteen-year-old brother was so badly beaten he could not pull his trousers up around his swollen legs. And then there was his friend Mapetla Mohape.

Mapetla was detained and charged with conspiring to recruit teens to fight against South Africa. He managed to smuggle out a note, written on toilet paper, to his wife, Nohle, Biko's secretary. In it he said the situation was bad but that he was OK. He would be back. And then two weeks later she was curtly informed that her husband had hanged himself from the bars of his police cell, with a pair of jeans.

Biko knew this was a lie. The police ascribed almost every death in detention to suicide. Soon after, Nohle herself was arrested. The police tried to bribe her to spy on Biko. They also tried to cajole her into attending meetings and workshops where she was supposed to record conversations and presentations.

Because she refused their orders, they detained her again and again. "The first month during my detention, I didn't get a drop of water to wash myself, I was unable to change, and I was in my menstrual cycle," she said as she later described her ordeal.

Her daughter, not yet four, cried and begged to be arrested so she could be with her mom. Unable to charge Biko, the police released him after a few months.

Back home, his personal life was in chaos. He and Ntsiki had had another boy, Samora, but she was no longer willing to overlook his relationship with Mamphela. She demanded he end his relationship with Mamphela, who had now been banned to the northernmost parts of the country, a small rural area called Tzaneen. Soon she wrote to him to say she was pregnant again.

Biko's time in prison only served to strengthen his commitment to the struggle. Soon after his release, he received a request to meet with Senator Dick Clark, the chairman of the US Senate Foreign Relations Committee's Subcommittee on Africa. Prior to the meeting, Biko had sent Clark a long memo in which he scathingly criticized the role of the United States in the "shameful history of our country."

He went on to define a set of minimum steps the Carter Administration should take, including sanctions and calling for the release of political prisoners like

Nelson Mandela. He also met frequently with the Australian diplomat, Bruce Haigh, who pressured the Australian government to take a strong anti-apartheid stance. Biko met with Ann Wilkens from the Swedish Ministry for Foreign Affairs at the Zanempilo clinic.

Essentially, Steve Biko's role in King William's Town was that of a statesman in waiting.

Perhaps the most important activity Biko was involved in was working on unifying the liberation movements, both inside and outside the country. The Black Consciousness movement had no offices or network outside the country, and the exodus of so many of its young followers was a problem. Most of the youngsters ended up with the ANC, although some found a home with the PAC. Biko knew it was urgent that the three organizations unite and coordinate their activities.

He had already sneaked out of Ginsberg to meet with Robert Sobukwe, the leader of the PAC, who himself was banned to Kimberley, a diamond-mining town in the heart of the country. Biko knew it was imperative he also meet with Oliver Tambo and the ANC. He planned on leaving South Africa secretly to travel to Lagos, Nigeria, where the UN World Conference for Action against Apartheid was to be held in late August 1977. There he would meet Tambo.

What was less well known is that Olof Palme, Sweden's ex-prime minister, would be a keynote speaker at the meeting, and should Biko attend the conference, he would likely also meet with Palme.

Olof Palme was Sweden's JFK; handsome, boyish-looking, and filled with heroic idealism. To many of his opponents, he was too emotional, almost tyrannical. To his admirers, he was a brilliant visionary who lived and breathed the dream for all people to be free.

Palme was convinced that the desire of black people for their freedom far outweighed their commitment to communism. He was known to say, "One of the reasons for our involvement [in the antiapartheid struggle] is to show that you do not have to be a communist to be against apartheid."

Under Palme, Sweden, more than all Western countries, became the most dependable humanitarian ally of the liberation movements in southern Africa. The author Tor Sellström estimated that Sweden alone contributed close on 4 billion Swedish kronor of humanitarian assistance to the liberation movements in southern Africa.

In early 1977, a few months after the Soweto Uprising, Palme denounced South Africa at the UN Security Council. "More than sixteen thousand bullets were fired in Soweto alone from June 16 to September 16. Eighty percent of those killed were shot in the back. A doctor at the Peninsula Maternity Hospital in Cape Town states that in his hospital alone seventy infants died from tear-gas poisoning." He concluded with a call for an arms and trade embargo and support for the liberation movements.

His next major speech against apartheid was to be in Africa, at the World Conference for Action against Apartheid in Lagos, Nigeria, when he would also meet with Biko and Oliver Tambo.

The meeting between Biko, Tambo, and Palme, if it took

place, could result in a formidable alliance between the youngest, most vibrant liberation movement, the oldest, most established one, and apartheid's most powerful and vocal enemy in the Western world. It would no doubt hasten the demise of apartheid.

15

IT WAS A WEEK BEFORE Steve Biko was to travel to Lagos. He and his friend Peter Jones were traveling in a Peugeot 504 station wagon. They were about an hour away from home.

Biko was way outside the district his banning order restricted him to. Peter Jones was driving, and Biko had his headphones on and was listening to a portable tape recorder on his lap. They were both relaxed and glad to be so close to home.

It was around 10:00 p.m. when Jones saw the blue flashing lights of a police roadblock up ahead. His heart hammering, he slowed down and stopped behind a red station wagon. He watched the policemen stride over and hoped they would wave him on. But his hopes sank when a policeman pulled his car out of the line. He demanded Jones open the trunk. Jones got out, his nerves rattled. He was unfamiliar with the car, which he had borrowed from a friend, and he struggled – and eventually failed – to open the lock.

Biko, who had remained seated, was ordered out of the car, too. The policemen searched the car and confiscated everything in it. Then they turned to search the men. They demanded Biko remove his belt. It had a large buckle, and Biko fumbled with it.

"Open it!" yelled one the policemen.

Biko stared at the man and said, "If you insist on being rude, you will get no cooperation from us. If, however, you choose to be more civil, you can be assured of our cooperation."

The officer smirked. "Just pray you never fall into my hands again."

In spite of his bravado, he didn't touch Biko again. They were both allowed to remove their own belts.

This was not the first time Biko had given his jailers "lip." During one of his previous spells in detention, he had punched a senior security officer who had slapped him across the face, busting the officer's teeth in the process.

On that evening in August, it is not clear whether the police manning the roadblock knew the passenger was Biko, but by the time they hauled the two men and their vehicle to the police station, they were in no doubt. They informed their senior commander, Piet Goosen, Williamson's handler.

Biko and Jones were locked in separate cells for the night.

The next morning, the two men were handcuffed and shoved into a police car. They were taken to room 619 on the sixth floor of the Sanlam Building.

There they were re-handcuffed but this time with one hand attached to the window bars. Security policemen walked in and out. They insulted and laughed at them. After a while the two men were uncuffed and taken down to the ground floor, where they were again separated.

Jones was told to lie face down on the floor between the seats of a van. He turned to look at Biko who had just passed behind him and called out his name.

Biko stopped. "Jones!" He smiled his gap-toothed smile at Jones and nodded a greeting. But within a few seconds they were both slapped violently and shoved into the vans.

Jones was taken to another police station where, over a period of days, he was "softened up." In frigid temperatures, he was stripped down and given a single blanket for warmth. Security policemen, never fewer than four, rushed into his cell every six hours or so, day and night. They screamed at him, woke him up, shoved him into icy cold showers, and taunted him. Deprivation of sleep and food were routine practices in the police handbook of torture. His first formal interrogation started a week later and lasted more than twenty hours. His interrogators alternated between lecturing him on why he had forsaken his coloured people and allowed himself to be used by the "*kaffirs*" and hitting him with a hosepipe fitted with a metal rod, demanding to know details of overseas funding and foreign visitors to King William's Town.

During the interrogation, still naked, he was made to stand on two bricks and hold two chairs above his head. He was beaten whenever he dropped the chairs. A week after his arrest, the police eased up slightly on the beatings. He was taken outside. "It was raining, and my shirt and jeans were lying on the cement in the water. I put these on. My request for shoes was refused."

Biko, on the other hand, was kept naked and chained in a cold cell for twenty days. His daily ration was soup, sour milk, bread, jam, and coffee. While his body contracted on the starvation diet, his mind stayed razor-sharp.

On the twenty-first day at around nine in the morning, he was ordered to dress and was brought again to room 619 in the Sanlam Building. He was handcuffed and in shackles. Major Snyman, head of the four-man interrogation team, gave instructions for his shackles to be removed. He ordered Biko to stay standing. Biko had no intention of cooperating. He ignored his interrogators, treating them as if they didn't exist, and sat down in a chair. Captain Siebert, Snyman's deputy, instructed Biko to remain standing. He ignored the command. Siebert yelled at the top of his voice for Biko to stand up. Biko continued to ignore him. Siebert then grabbed him by his clothes and pulled him upright. Biko lunged at Siebert and tried to land a punch on his face.

Enraged by Biko's insolence, five policemen the size of rugby players tackled him. They struggled to subdue the hefty Biko. Finally, infuriated, they ran him into a wall, slamming his head against the concrete.

As with Nazi bureaucracy, at every level of apartheid's administration there existed a systematic brutality and cruelty that culminated in Biko's death. It started with the policemen who slammed his head into the wall, and was escalated by those who ignored the glazed and confused look in his eyes and shackled him "crucifixion-style" to the grille and then kept him in chains even after his hands, feet, and ankles were swollen and cut.

Then two doctors saw him during their lunch break and ignored his urine-soaked trousers and his obvious brain injury and kidney failure. The prison hospital warders observed a confused Biko get into a bath fully clothed and yet permitted his return from the prison hospital to a cold prison cell.

Piet Goosen commanded his unit to transport the half-comatose Biko—on a frigid winter night, alone, naked, and in shackles—in the back of a van from Port Elizabeth to Pretoria, a journey that took more than ten hours. Goosen later spun the web of lies to absolve himself and his department. All of this civilized barbarity was possible because Steve Biko was a black man and therefore, in their eyes, less than human.

Stephen Bantu Biko died in the month of September, called EyoMsintsi in traditional Xhosa society, the month of the coastal coral tree, when the coral trees in his hometown glow with their springtime fire-colored flowers. He was thirty years old, having started a movement at the age of twenty that changed the course of his country. He was the twenty-first political detainee to die in detention in South Africa since the Soweto Uprising, a little over one year before.

Biko's coffin, the lid bearing the emblem of the Black Consciousness movement in iron, a carving of two hands breaking shackles, rested overnight in mamCethe's cottage in Ginsberg. The next day, a blustery Sunday, two days after the spring equinox, the coffin was laid on a trailer to which were yoked two oxen. In an honor reserved only for chiefs and

Xhosa royalty, the trailer inched its journey of more than a mile to the stadium where a massive crowd had assembled.

In the largest political funeral rally seen up to that time, an estimated ten thousand people came to mourn Biko. Many thousands were prevented from reaching the funeral at roadblocks, where they were hauled off buses and assaulted by the police. Thirteen Western nations sent diplomats to the funeral, including Sweden, Norway, Finland, and the Carter Administration in the United States.

The crowd, angry and restless, broke out into "Nkosi Sikelel' iAfrika" as the oxen pulled into the stadium grounds. But above the anger could be heard the mournful crying of Samora, Biko's younger son who was still a toddler. Biko had been detained a few days after Samora's birthday, and the child missed his father so much he still ran to the phone, expecting to hear his dad's voice.

Close to a thousand miles away, Biko's girlfriend, Mamphela, banned in Tzaneen, was in hospital. She was bleeding from a threatened miscarriage. Their son, Hlumelo, was born a few months later.

The newspaper report of Steve Biko's death was as an article no larger than the size of a credit card. Years later my brother said to me, "I remember clearly where I was when I saw that article, at home, in our lounge. My heart jumped when I read it. It was so small but I knew everything was about to change."

In the weeks after Biko's funeral, Prime Minister Vorster ordered the arrest of hundreds of activists, banned all Black Consciousness organizations and many black newspapers, and outlawed all open-air gatherings.

Peter Jones was released a year and a half after his arrest.

The ramifications of Steve Biko's death blew across South Africa like an arctic chill. But his philosophy had wound its way into the hearts and minds of South Africans.

PART 3

16

A WEEK BEFORE THE CHRISTMAS OF 1979, a dark-haired man in his thirties, wearing a black turtleneck, landed at Heathrow Airport. He made his way through the crowds toward immigration. His name was Arthur McGiven, and he was a BOSS spy and a colleague of Craig Williamson's. But McGiven was an angry spy, the worst kind. He was angry at his colleagues in BOSS who harassed him when they found out he lived with a man. In his briefcase, he carried documents that proved the apartheid government had tapped into the conversations of British members of Parliament and intercepted the mail of prominent CEOs and directors of mining companies, activities that went far beyond simple security measures.

The London Sunday newspaper, the *Observer,* ran the scoop.

For the first time, the usually unflappable Williamson

was rattled. McGiven's evidence was damning, and it was a question of time before Williamson was exposed and arrested. He knew that spying on foreign officials would afford him little sympathy in a European court of law.

Late at night he went to the IUEF offices and cleared out his desk, as well as documents from the safe. He fled Geneva for London, where his mentor Johan Coetzee met him. The two made a last-ditch unsuccessful effort to blackmail Eriksson, Williamson's boss at the aid agency, into keeping Williamson on.

A few days later, a relieved Williamson, disguised as an old man, boarded a plane. Shuffling and helped by a cabin attendant, he escaped back to South Africa.

Although his time as a spy had been short-lived, Craig Williamson learned valuable lessons in Cold War tactics, including how to set up and manage offshore banking accounts and "front companies" designed to hide the covert work of the apartheid government.

He had succeeded in diverting hundreds of thousands in foreign aid money away from the liberation organizations into apartheid coffers, as well as fingering a number of people who were tried and imprisoned. But he had failed in his primary mission to infiltrate the ANC and SACP. The main reason for the failure was not the McGiven affair but Jeanette and Marius Schoon. The two teachers, working in Botswana, became suspicious of Williamson after he had stayed with them on a number of occasions. They warned senior members in the ANC, who kept Williamson at arm's length.

Within days of his return, the apartheid propaganda machine swung into action and Williamson was lauded in the state-run media as the "super spy" who had infiltrated deep into the ANC, accolades that would be useful in the next stage of his career with South Africa's covert agencies.

But all was not victory parades and streamers for Williamson. His exposure and return to the country occurred on the heels of the ousting of Vorster and van den Bergh. It wasn't the mowing down of hundreds of children or even the murder of Steve Biko that brought the pair down, but the waste of public funds highlighted by the Infogate scandal that awakened the anger of white voters. Over a period of five years, the Vorster government had spent more than $70 million on propaganda to influence world opinion in favor of South Africa. This included bribing foreign journalists to write favorable articles about the country, buying ailing newspapers like the *Washington Star* and *Sacramento Union,* and funding luxury safaris for American congressmen. Eschel Rhoodie, a whistle-blower, claimed Vorster had approved spending $250,000 to help defeat Senator Dick Clark.

Vorster was replaced by the dour-faced, grouchy P. W. Botha, his minister of defense. Botha was paranoid the communist threat had infiltrated the country, and in his mind, this "total onslaught" required nothing less than a "total strategy," both national and international.

Assassination became a key tool of Botha's state policy. At secret meetings, the Sanhedrin, a body of men at the highest level, selected targets for elimination through direct kidnappings and shooting, poisoning, and letter bombs.

In this new climate, Williamson's cunning stood him in good stead. He played down his association with van den Bergh's BOSS and highlighted his work for the security branch of the police. He was a master strategist and knew he could leverage his knowledge of the command structures of the liberation organizations. Soon he was appointed to the Sanhedrin.

In 1981, with the inauguration of Ronald Reagan, and with Margaret Thatcher in power in the United Kingdom, Botha had all he needed to put in place the campaigns that would make the eighties apartheid's most vicious decade.

More than any other leader before him, he would head a security apparatus that would detain and kill thousands of children, students whose primary demand was a free, compulsory, and democratic education.

17

THE GROOM, TSIETSI MASHININI, WAS tall and slim. He wore a white suit and sported a goatee. The bride, Welma Campbell, Miss Liberia 1977, was breathtaking. She had high cheekbones and a fresh, honest smile, and she looked angelic in a cap-sleeved gown of white lace, and delicate jewelry.

Tsietsi and Welma were married in January 1979, at the American Methodist Episcopal Church in Monrovia, the cultural, political, and financial hub of Liberia on the west coast of Africa.

After the wedding, the couple and their guests moved on to a beach resort for their reception. They chatted with their three hundred or so guests, whom Tsietsi charmed with his easy banter. Miriam Makeba mesmerized the crowd with her white smile, sparkling eyes, and "Pata Pata," her hit song from the sixties. Dazzling in her African-print outfit and beaded braids, she swung her hips gently as she sang the tongue-twisting clicks of the Xhosa song.

But Tsietsi felt acutely the absence of his beloved family and friends.

Life in exile had been exciting for a while. He and his friends were honored as heroes. His bold ideas, his intensity, and his charisma drew followers as he traveled through the United States and the United Kingdom, where he was interviewed by top newspapers and spoke at meetings and conferences. He was convinced he would return soon, as a young leader, to a free South Africa.

But as the initial excitement wore off and reality set in, he struggled to find his place in this new world where no country felt like home. Leaders of the ANC had offered their help and arranged a speaking tour for the young man to raise money for the child refugees back in Botswana. But Tsietsi felt used. He felt the ANC was taking credit for the Soweto Uprising, when in fact, it was the Black Consciousness movement that had been the real force behind it.

He was a natural risk taker, convinced he was the master of his own destiny. But the life of an exile during the Cold War era required discipline. It required him to put in time as a follower, and patiently wait out the years until he would become a leader. Tsietsi had no tolerance for such a life.

He began to believe he needed to start his own liberation army but found it almost impossible to raise funds and make any headway against the ANC, which had spent many decades establishing itself as the premier liberation movement. He lost his temper often, and his angry outbursts made him insufferable even to his closest friends.

And then he met Welma. She came from a well-known Liberian family. Her father was a lawyer and her mother a congresswoman.

At the wedding, Tsietsi missed his mother the most. Her unwavering love and support had sustained him throughout his youth. He missed his father's sturdy presence and his brothers and baby sisters, but also his friends, most of whom he had lost touch with and not invited to his wedding.

Over the next few years, Tsietsi and Welma had two little girls, whom they named Nomkhitha and Thembi. But he remained rudderless, hopping from country to country, all the while trying to raise money for an armed insurrection.

Elsewhere in the country, a new generation of high school students, the younger brothers and sisters of the June 16 generation, politicized by the events they had experienced a few years before, stepped forward to continue the struggle. This time it was the coloured students from the sprawling low-income housing of the Cape Flats who took up the baton.

Many of the families in the Cape Flats originally lived in the center of Cape Town in District 6, a vibrant community of artists, merchants, and immigrants. Some of District 6 residents were sixth-generation descendants of Muslim slaves who were exiled to South Africa for stoking revolution in the colonies of the Dutch East Indies. Thus the people of District 6 were a mixed bag of DNA—Malay, European, Indian, Khoisan, and West African. Determined to classify this group, the apartheid government coined the term "Cape Coloured."

Over a period of years during the seventies, in its attempt to make Cape Town a whites-only zone, the government shattered the community of District 6 and forced its residents into box houses in the Cape Flats.

In 1980, on a sunny morning in April, the children of the Cape Flats decided to voice their demands for an equal education.

William Finnegan, a *New Yorker* author, working as a teacher in the Cape Flats at the time, described the morning the protests began. "The entire student body was marching in a great solid phalanx around the campus, chanting, carrying placards, singing freedom songs... The Grassy Park faculty trailed behind the children in a knot, looking nervous... Students of mine waved excitedly from the midst of the marching column, as though they had just boarded a train bound for somewhere wonderful, and I was on the platform seeing them off. A colleague pointed out a white car parked across the street from the school. 'The Special Branch,' he hissed. One of the two men in the car was taking pictures."

The students had had enough. Enough of the army recruits who were assigned to teach them. Enough of the Hippos on their school grounds. Enough of the lack of stationery and textbooks. Enough of not being able to elect their school prefects and class representatives, the principals appointing them instead. Enough of the system that was still rigged to allow only a small number of them to graduate from high school. Enough of the unofficial passing curve at every grade level that forced those who failed to become fodder for the massive unskilled-labor market.

But this time the students were better prepared than in 1976. They elected a group to coordinate and negotiate on their behalf, the Committee of 81. They detailed specific demands, both near - and long-term. They looked for support from their parents and teachers.

They aligned their efforts with the workers' struggle by raising money for workers who had been fired for striking. They threw their weight behind the bus boycott—minimum wage workers spent almost a quarter of their salaries on bus fares and the increases hit them hard.

They devised an alternative curriculum, which, according to Finnegan, included "computers, women's issues, sex and contraception, the French Revolution, the Bolshevik Revolution, Khoisan culture, the government's planned bantustan [reservations for blacks] policy, and the tradition of black resistance."

Again the school boycotts spread throughout the country. In a matter of months, more than a hundred thousand black students were boycotting school.

The boycott initially involved mainly coloured and Indian students, but as weeks passed, African students as well as university students at the "bush" colleges (derisive term for blacks-only colleges) joined in.

Music was an important part of the boycotts. Pink Floyd's hit, "Another Brick in the Wall Part 2," was released a few months before the boycott began. To the students, it felt as if the song with its hypnotic beat and explosive lyrics was written just for them, and the chorus of actual schoolchildren in the song was them.

We don't need no education
We don't need no thought control
No dark sarcasm, in the classroom

Teachers, leave them kids alone
Hey! Teacher! Leave those kids alone
All in all you're just another brick in the wall.

Then the government banned the song. No one was allowed to sell or possess the song, and certainly no one could play it in public. The song went underground. It was still played on millions of cassette players in townships throughout the country. In public the children rewrote the lyrics.

We want equal facilities
We don't need no forced control
Hey! Cops! Leave us kids alone
All in all it's just another peaceful protest.

By Monday, June 16, the four-year anniversary of the Soweto Uprising, the students had still not returned to class.

In almost every major city and town in South Africa, massive numbers of black students, workers, and shoppers heeded a call for a two-day boycott, designed to bring the economy to a grinding halt as a form of protest.

In Cape Town, the day started off peacefully, but within hours skirmishes between the students and the police broke out. Mattresses, old cars, burning tires, tree branches, chicken-wire fencing all contributed to the massive barricades the students had erected to disrupt traffic flow from the city to its main international airport in Cape Town. The streets became giant battlefields with students pelting police with stones.

In this pandemonium, police sharpshooters began to pick off individuals randomly.

Forty-two people were killed in the Cape Flats over the two days. Over two hundred people were injured and many were women and children.

After much debate, the coloured and Indian schools ended their participation in the boycott by July. The government had gone into a frenzy of detentions. Most of the members of the organizing committee were arrested. The remaining members of the committee went into hiding. African schools, especially in the Eastern Cape, the region of Steve Biko's hometown, continued their boycott until August.

The boycotts had, however, raised a generation of politicized students. There was no going back. Over the next few years, the student uprising became a full-fledged movement and eventually a critical pillar in the struggle against apartheid.

18

It was 1981, and Johannesburg was covered in snow. Close to four inches of slushy, wet snow. It was the heaviest snowfall recorded in the history of the city.

Ours was one of a few homes on the edge of downtown Johannesburg. We lived less than four blocks away from major banks and shopping stores. My dad believed, incorrectly as luck would have it, that the city would move toward our house and he would be able to sell at a huge profit. But because Indians were not allowed to own property in Johannesburg, although he paid for the property, on paper a trusted colleague of his, a white man, owned fifty-one percent of the property.

The area was a strange no-man's land, being a business district it emptied out on weekends and public holidays. We had no neighborhood as such and no social clubs, parks or soccer fields. I grew up reading books and comics to pass the time.

But only a few streets away, white Johannesburg was a magical place. Born hurriedly out of the gold rush a century before, it had bloomed into the financial capital of the country and the richest city in all of Africa. It was like a miniature London, but less crowded and with more sunshine. The City Hall, a great Edwardian building with its magnificent sixthousand-pipe organ dominated the center of the downtown district. Elegant department stores like John Orr's, Greatermans and Stuttafords, surrounded it. Well-dressed white women sipped tea at little cafés after shopping or visiting their dressmaker. They may even have time to attend a lunchtime concert at the City Hall.

At Christmas time the city transformed into a fairytale place. It came to life, with thousands of lights and the jingle of Christmas songs. A red double-decker bus, decorated like a well-lit Christmas tree, ferried children back and forth along the main streets. OK Bazaars put on an enchanting pantomime on its balcony and the bronze statue of a herd of Impala flying through a misty fountain in the center of downtown gave the city an ethereal quality.

As I grew up I realized that in this fascinating mosaic of everyday life lay the reasons why apartheid thrived for so many decades. While the government apparatus put in place the legal framework for apartheid, the Dutch Reformed Church gave the policy a sense of divine approval: bureaucratic and security minions enforced it, private business, the gold and diamond mines, the farms all flourished from it, and everyday whites enjoyed the fruits and security it brought them.

We blacks were banished to being the orphans peering in through the windows. The Christmas bus was for whites only. The ice rink at the top of the Carlton Centre was for whites only. The restaurants were for whites only. The park benches in Oppenheimer Park where white toddlers chased pigeons and the impalas flew over the mist, were for whites only. Most of the jobs were for whites only. Blacks were allowed to do menial work in the city but not allowed to own any property. Africans had to carry their *dompas* around all the time and were expected to be out of the city after dark. While young white girls stepped lightly through the streets in their miniskirts and sparkling white knee-high boots, African men would stand on the street corner and wolf down a packet of cookies with a soda to keep to the fifteen minute lunch break they were allowed.

So, that September, when it snowed, we ran out onto the pavement to make a snowman. Passersby, mostly African men, stopped to help us construct our sad, rather weepy snowman, whom we dressed with my grandfather's gray felt hat and walking stick.

The next day I sat my pediatric exams. The hall was freezing, with no central heating and snow still on the ground. About an hour into the four-hour exam I needed to pee. But I had to finish the exam. I shook my legs and wiggled in my seat and completed the exam. By the time I got to the bathroom I was almost in tears from the pain of a bursting bladder.

A day later it felt like I was peeing razor blades. I had a urinary tract infection. I saw our family doctor, Dr. Essop Jassat.

"Hello Poppy, what's wrong?" he said. He gazed at me across the desk with his crinkly eyes, a gentle smile on his lips.

I burst into tears. He prescribed antibiotics and lots of water. Within a week my infection had cleared

Dr. Jassat wasn't only my doctor; he was also a

dedicated activist who came from a family of freedom fighters. His brother, Abdulhay Jassat, had joined an Umkhonto cell, which had placed a number of bombs aimed at destroying electrical pylons and other hard targets. Abdulhay was arrested, tortured with a soggy hessian bag over his head, and had 220 volts of electricity passed through his body through electrodes on his toes. Eventually Abdulhay had escaped and gone into exile where he was diagnosed with epilepsy, a result of brain injury sustained during the torture.

Abdulhay's experience had a huge impact on his younger brother, Essop, my doctor.

Until 1961, the apartheid government had always planned on repatriating Indians back to India, even though many generations of virtually all Indians in the country had been born in South Africa. Finally, in 1961, Indians were accepted as an official race group in the country.

A few compliant Indians were invited to form a body, the South African Indian Council (SAIC), a generally toothless, advisory body, that would serve as a link between the government and the Indian community. In general, Indians rejected these "leaders" of the SAIC as puppets of the government.

In 1981, for the first time the apartheid government set a date for elections to the SAIC. It was a watershed moment because a significant turnout would legitimize the SAIC and irrevocably divide the Indian struggle from that of Africans and coloureds.

Dr. Jassat was elected chairperson of the Transvaal Anti-SAIC Committee (TASC). My dad was already a member of the executive of TASC. My brothers and I joined them and the growing group of activists who canvassed door-to-door to convince people to boycott the elections. But there was one day of the week when we could not canvas at all. It was Tuesdays, the day when the TV soap opera *Dallas* aired. On a Tuesday, when J R Ewing, the oil tycoon with the devil eyebrows, was gracing their TV screens, no one would open their doors for us.

Nevertheless, the boycott was a huge success. The turnout was abysmal, and in our area it was close to a mere one percent.

19

IN LATE FEBRUARY 1982, CRAIG Williamson and his immediate superior, now known as Piet "Biko" Goosen, traveled to London with six members of his team. Their purpose was to plant a bomb.

The men traveled separately, in groups of two, using false names. The bomb was built into a radio and smuggled into the country via diplomatic luggage inside deodorant spray cans designed with the Playboy bunny logo.

Elsewhere in London, a tall man dressed in a purple cassock, Archbishop Trevor Huddleston, worked feverishly to organize the largest antiapartheid demonstration since Sharpeville in 1960. Hundreds of people, including heads of governments and liberation movements, leaders of the British Labour and Liberal parties, and representatives of churches, trade unions, student organizations, and women's groups were to attend an ambitious four-day conference titled "Southern Africa: Time to Choose." The conference was to end on Sunday with a massive rally in Trafalgar Square, in front of the South African embassy.

Roger Raven, Williamson's bomb maker, booked a flight to Frankfurt for his escape and then went to various hardware stores to buy a soldering iron, metal shears, radio wire, batteries, and two Timex watches. He also purchased dark clothing, running shoes, a balaclava, and a bag.

In a two-story house in a London suburb, he assembled the deadly device. At ten in the evening, the day before the march, the men planted the bomb, housed in a large green sports bag. It had close to ten pounds of explosives, and when detonated it could cause damage within a radius of more than 150 feet.

Their job completed, the men left the scene and gave their shoes, gloves, and balaclavas to Williamson, who threw them into the River Thames.

The next morning, the day of the march, the bomb went off as thousands of people began to stream into the center of London.

The Guardian newspaper reported, "The London offices of the African National Congress were wrecked by a 10-pound bomb which exploded against the rear wall at nine o'clock yesterday morning. Windows up to 400 yards away were shattered."

An ANC volunteer who was sleeping in the building was injured. The windows of the White Lion Free School next door were totally shattered by the blast.

Over the next few years, Williamson sent letter bombs to a number of targets. Having convinced himself all anti-apartheid activists were the enemy, he had no hesitation in selecting "soft" targets.

He had Roger Raven post a bomb to Mozambique, where it killed Ruth First, who was everything the

Afrikaners despised. She was a brave and intelligent white woman who was also a dedicated Marxist. One of the first investigative journalists in the country, she was the "liberation publicist" of the anti-apartheid movement, and wife of Joe Slovo, head of the South African Communist Party, who was regarded by the apartheid government as the "evil genius" behind many acts of sabotage carried out within South Africa by Umkhonto.

In a few years Williamson would turn his focus on Jeanette and Marius Schoon.

20

I was fresh out of Wits, idealistic, ready to take on the world as I began my medical internship. It was January when I drove into Baragwanath Hospital in Soweto. I remember the sun shining through the window, warming my arm, and the cool breeze ruffling my hair. The car was my dad's 1970 Mercedes-Benz, and my brothers had dubbed it 'Mr. Mukerjee', as if it were an aging Bollywood star. Mr. Mukerjee had aged ungracefully and had developed a tendency to backfire, which was the only sound that broke that morning's peace.

Thus, all eyes were on Mr. Mukerjee and me as I drove through the gates and into the parking lot of the sprawling hospital that was to become my second home for the remainder of the year.

It was a year that transformed me, during which I saw the most vulnerable side of humanity and during which I marveled at the resilience of the human spirit.

There was newly married Grace, admitted to the emergency room after vomiting up five cupfuls of fresh blood. She had lupus, an auto-immune disease. When we started her on steroids I was so naïve I told her husband, "She's going to be better now." I still remember him nodding and smiling gratefully at me. The next day as I walked into the ward, one of my fellow interns told me Grace had died from a massive gastrointestinal hemorrhage during the night. I stared at him, blinking furiously, trying to make sense of his words. And then I ran out. I drove to the farthest corner of the hospital complex and wept for Grace and my own stupidity. Two days later I had to attend her autopsy.

There was Joyce, a mother of three, all under the age of five. A paraffin-fuelled fridge exploded just as she leaned over to examine it. The skin on Joyce's chin, neck, chest, and arms, except for her face and hands was scorched. For three months Joyce lay motionless on the hospital bed, all the joints on her upper body outstretched to allow the skin grafts to take hold without scarring, which would have limited movements of her joints. The nurses and I arranged for a donated Disney-princess mirror to be placed next to her bed so she could see what was happening in the ward. I bought her favorite romance novels, which the nurses read to her. In all that time, she refused to allow her husband to bring her children to visit her. I never once heard her complain or cry or whine. When she returned for her outpatient visit, her two-year-old daughter clung to her, absolutely refusing to get off her hip. I had to examine Joyce with her youngest child still attached to her.

Then there was Henry, a schizophrenic. He was my favorite patient, and I was his favorite intern. He was brought—shouting and screaming, possessed by unseen demons—into an already busy and understaffed emergency room, where twenty nurses and doctors served a community of a million people. Restrained on a gurney by an unknown attendant until someone could attend to him, he was tied down tightly, just below the elbows, for an unknown period of time. His admission notes went missing soon after. His gangrenous arm, dry, discolored, and skeletal, required amputation, and I was assigned to work him up for surgery.

One day, after our grand ward round, as the entire surgical team walked toward our respective white or black doctors' tearooms, I heard Henry calling my name. There he was, running stark naked, his flaccid penis swinging wildly with each step. "Your patient's looking for you," the head of our unit said. I blushed a deep red, and amid the giggles of my fellow interns, I took Henry's arm, and we shuffled back to the ward.

By the end of the year, I was exhausted and ready for a change. I made an appointment to see Professor Welsh, the new head of ophthalmology at Wits. I wanted to specialize in ophthalmology, but I also knew it was in great demand. "You need to pass the surgical part 1 exam before you'll get into ophthalmology," he said.

I passed the exam, but a couple of years later I learned the requirement was only for black doctors. White doctors were not expected to pass the exam before being admitted to the department. I wasn't surprised that rules were fluid. Angry, yes, but not surprised. In fact, as an ophthalmologist I also learned that whites were not above accepting the corneas harvested from dead black patients when it came to organ transplants.

21

MARIUS AND JEANETTE SCHOON WERE now in Lubango, Angola. They had had to flee their home in Botswana. Their second child, Fritz, had just turned three, and Katryn was six.

Botswana had become intolerable. Soon after Craig Williamson had been exposed, an uneasiness had worked its way into their everyday lives. The incidents were relatively minor but had a cumulative effect.

Money was always tight. They managed by taking on various teaching jobs at high schools or universities.

In June 1983, Botswana's head of security informed them he had reliable intelligence information that Marius was to be assassinated. Within days, the ANC head office in Lusaka sent instructions for the entire family to be redeployed immediately.

Marius flew to Lusaka, and Jeanette drove with the kids, accompanied by her brother. They reached Lusaka safely, but a few months later they found themselves transferred again—this time to Lubango, in Angola.

Lubango lay in the war zone that separated Cuban and Angolan troops from South African forces.

Since the mid-seventies, tens of thousands of

Cubans, military and civilian, had volunteered to serve in Angola. They were there to fight the apartheid government and its ally, the United States, in the proxy Cold War that raged for more than two decades in that oil - and mineral-rich country.

Jeanette and Marius were assigned to the university in Lubango. She was to teach English to first - and second-year students, and he was to teach linguistics to third-year students.

At the time they arrived in Lubango, the South African Defence Force had yet again invaded Angola. Soldiers patrolled the streets all the time. Food was exceptionally scarce, and it was difficult to get water.

They didn't speak Portuguese or Spanish, and there were only two other South Africans in the town. Nightly shootings were the norm, and Cuban helicopters flew day and night, more or less at the level of their balcony.

On a Thursday, the letter bomb prepared by Raven and sent by Craig Williamson arrived at the apartment of the Schoon family.

Jeanette and Katryn were killed immediately. When Marius, who was away on a trip, returned home, little Fritz, who had been playing outside the apartment when the bomb exploded, hugged his father and cried, "They broke Jenny."

PART 4

22

If, in 1984, P. W. Botha thought he was winning the war against the "total onslaught," by 1985 the tide began to turn against him. Within the country, a grassroots movement was stealthily spreading.

Two years before, in a Cape Town community hall, delegates from dozens of organizations gathered to launch the United Democratic Front (UDF).

While hundreds of youngsters bobbed up and down and chanted slogans, a little girl in a pink gingham dress and braided pigtails stood up to speak. Her name was Leila Issel. The crowd hushed as Leila's voice, soft and shy, rang out. "My daddy cannot be here because he's banned. My daddy supports the UDF because he wants to see us free. He believes freedom will come in our lifetime." She looked up self-consciously from the paper in her hand and smiled at the crowd.

The gathering was the national launch of the United

Democratic Front (UDF). Formed to defy Botha's prized Tricameral Parliament, which was made up of three separate parliaments for whites, Indians, and coloureds.

But the number of seats in the white parliament far outnumbered the total number of seats in the Indian and coloured parliaments. No Africans were allowed to vote in these parliaments. Instead, Africans were assigned to their separate bantustans (reservations).

Atop the multicolored house of cards would preside the State President, a post created for himself by P. W. Botha, dubbed 'the Great Crocodile' by the press. The new constitution stated that the President would not be controlled by the courts or by parliament, and in fact would have the final say over all decisions by parliament, as well as having total authority to dissolve any of the three houses of parliament.

In the Rocklands Civic Centre, the hall was festooned with banners that bore the names of hundreds of organizations, from women's groups, to trade unions, to rent associations, to doctors' groupings, and of course to student and youth organizations. The canary yellow and red UDF banners lit up the stage. Hundreds of youngsters, standing around the periphery of the room, bobbed up and down and chanted, "UDF. UDF, UDF!"

Archie Gumede, one of the three presidents of the new organization said, "Apartheid must be banished from the face of South Africa... To slogans must be added sweat. To those slogans must be added labor, and careful thought and careful action."

The crowd roared repeatedly, "Archie Gumm-meeeede! Hai... Hai, hai."

Aubrey Mokoena, who had been arrested and banned for his involvement in Biko's SASO, and whose five-year banning order had just expired, spoke, "Brothers and sisters, the struggle is marching on.... We have come here to energize ourselves. To be charged at the terminals of this battery. And then we go back, to form branches of UDF throughout the country... to build the image of UDF, to popularize UDF. To set up meaningful community projects."

The crowd reserved the most resounding ovation for an elegant white woman who wore her gray hair in a small bun. Helen Joseph had dedicated her life to end apartheid. In 1956 she, with others, had spearheaded the march of 20,000 women on Pretoria. In the same year she was arrested, and stood trial with Nelson Mandela and more than a hundred and fifty others, during the Treason Trial. She was acquitted but banned immediately. The order was renewed again and again, to be finally lifted only when she was eighty. The diminutive Ms. Joseph received a standing ovation lasting many minutes.

The booming voice of the young Reverend Alan Boesak resounded across the room. "We are here to say that there are rights.... They are God-given. And so we are here not to beg for those rights, but we are here to claim them."

After reminding whites that their destiny was "inexplicably bound" with the destiny of blacks, Allen Boesak closed the conference. "Brothers and sisters let me remind you of three little words. Three little words that express so eloquently our seriousness in the struggle. Just three little words. The first word is ALL... We want all of our rights for all of South

Africa's people. The second word is the word HERE. We want all of our rights and we want them here. In a unified, undivided South Africa. We don't want them in the impoverished homelands, we want them here in this land we call our home. And the third word is the word NOW. We want all our rights, and we want them here and we want them now!"

By the time Boesak finished his last sentence, every person in the hall was standing up, their fists clenched and raised. A thundering male voice broke out into "Nkosi Sikelel' iAfrika" and more than a thousand voices chorused.

Outside the hall, the police had set up watch posts and were taking photographs of the participants. But the crowd was unfazed. A few hours later, the conference was followed by a rally attended by more than 15,000 people. They ranged across all age groups, all colors, all ethnicities, all religions.

Thus, in response to the Tricameral Parliament, the three black race groups united against Botha. In the next two years, under its slogan "UDF Unites, Apartheid Divides", the UDF consolidated people across race groups, and spread its roots, like a stubborn weed, into virtually every black community. Its membership was estimated to be close to three million people. White organizations like the End Conscription Campaign, formed to defy the draft for white males, found a home in the UDF. The pillars of the movement were the trade unions, the women's and civic organizations, and the youth movement.

The youth movement included hundreds of youth

groups and clubs, but the largest was the Congress of South African Students (COSAS). When the student boycotts occurred in 1980, COSAS was still a fledgling organization. In the years since, it had matured into a fully developed national movement with a multipronged strategy. It boasted a million members, with millions of supporters.

The students defined an education charter. Government and big business colluded to dilute the effect of the movement by having businesses "adopt" black schools and provide a few computers and TVs in the vain hope that students would forget their demands. But the education charter went a long way in keeping students focused. It also became a way to judge concessions made by the government.

Frustrated, the government tried to clamp down on the movement through arrests. But to avoid collapse of their orgnanization, the youth had trained layers of leaders who could step in if others were arrested.

Students who were detained found themselves expelled and unable to find work. Their abuse at the hands of security police and their experiences after release left them bitter. They formed civic organizations that worked hand in hand with their fellow students to connect schools with their communities.

The students devised strategies to link the education struggle with the struggle of workers and civic organizations. Slogans like "People's Education for People's Power" linked democracy in schools with democracy in society. The COSAS leaders sent out questionnaires to branches, asking how strong their relationships with workers and community organizations were and their strategy to expand these connections.

Outside South Africa's borders, the anti-apartheid movement had grown into arguably one of the largest social justice movements of the twentieth century. Dozens of countries and millions of people all over the world committed themselves to ending apartheid.

By the early eighties, sports and consumer boycotts were widespread, and the United Nations had passed an arms embargo on South Africa.

The countries that were unfailing in their support for the liberation movement—and undoubtedly paid the highest price—were the African nations immediately surrounding South Africa. Called the Frontline States, these countries provided refuge for people fleeing apartheid and allowed liberation movements to open their offices within their borders. The South African Defence Force often invaded or bombed these countries, and in Mozambique and Angola, the apartheid government armed and trained rebel movements that totally destabilized these budding democracies. Farther away, countries like India, with deep connections through shared ancestries, tirelessly supported the struggle against apartheid. Among the Western nations, the Nordic countries, especially Sweden, remained firm in their humanitarian assistance as well as their commitment to ending apartheid through putting pressure Botha's government.

But the United States, the United Kingdom, and France remained unconvinced. Their attitude toward

Botha's government was one of "They're bad guys, but they're our bad guys."

By 1985 however, on apartheid at least, both Reagan (US President) and Thatcher (UK Prime Minister) had slipped out of sync with the people of their respective countries.

In America, groups such as the Congressional Black Caucus, TransAfrica, and the American Committee on Africa had worked for decades to raise awareness at the grassroots level. They petitioned the World Bank to stop loans to South Africa, they organized consumer boycotts of South African goods, and workers from the International Longshore and Warehouse Union in San Francisco refused to unload what they called "bloody" cargo from South Africa.

Under the Free South Africa campaign, a picket line in front of the South African embassy in Washington, DC, became a daily event. Police began to arrest everyday Americans and celebrities alike. They spent a night in jail before being bailed out. Even the famed American civil rights activist Rosa Parks joined the line. Over the course of a little more than a year, more than forty-five hundred people were arrested nationwide in the United States.

The student divestment movement on American campuses joined in and became a national movement with thousands of students demanding their college administrations stop investing college funds in companies that did business with the apartheid government. Many campuses built "shantytowns" on the lawns of their colleges to demonstrate the living conditions of South Africa's poor. Over a period of a few years close to 150 US campuses divested more than $3.5 billion out of companies investing in South Africa.

Spurred by the groundswell of protests, the Congressional Black Caucus tried to pass the Comprehensive Anti-Apartheid Act that would impose sanctions on South Africa.

Although Reagan vetoed the bill, the threat of sanctions by the United States meant other countries might soon follow. It resulted in a flight of capital from South Africa, and Botha's government found itself paying an extraordinary price for apartheid.

In Sweden, Olof Palme, who had been voted back into office in 1982, remained steadfast in his undertaking to end apartheid. To him there was no middle ground; he believed neutrality with regard to apartheid was impossible.

In a speech in 1984, he said, "The system of apartheid is and remains a moral outrage. It is the only system branding a person right from birth according to the color of their skin...This makes apartheid a tyranny of a particularly evil kind. Every civilized person and civilized people [society] must view it with contempt. It is our duty to eradicate this weird aberration in human history from the face of the earth."

Palme had a particular gift in finding the humanity in situations. He used simple examples to drive his point home. "Apartheid South Africa is in fact a society in permanent violence. Every three days a black man is hanged. Every year hundreds of thousands are arrested as a result of the pass laws. And every year close to one million Africans are brought to trial for violation of laws that apply to black people only."

With every speech he made, he pushed a three-pronged strategy of providing humanitarian aid to liberation movements, isolating South Africa, and applying sanctions against Botha's government.

Ordinary Swedes, regardless of political affiliation, responded to his call.

23

THOUSANDS OF MILES AWAY, THE youth of South Africa were locked in battle with their government. And one man integral to their struggle was Matthew Goniwe.

Goniwe was born a year after Steve Biko, in a town called Cradock in the vast, semi-arid region called the Great Karoo. It was here that he first attended school and dreamed of becoming a teacher. Skinny, with horn-rimmed glasses, he played rugby and loved music. He revered his older brother, Jacques, who was the first person in Cradock to burn his *dompas* (compulsory ID document) during the Defiance Campaign of the fifties. Jacques went into exile in 1960 and was killed trying to establish a route for the ANC in what was then called Rhodesia. His death had a huge impact on politicizing his younger brother.

Goniwe graduated as a science and math teacher from the University of Fort Hare, Nelson Mandela's alma mater. He loved teaching, and he knew a quality education was essential for blacks to take their place in a democratic South Africa. But to receive an education, his students needed to attend school. He often felt he was too much of a disciplinarian, but that didn't stop him visiting them at home to drag them back to school.

He married a young social worker, Nyameka, in 1975, and their baby was born soon after.

It was in the academic atmosphere of Fort Hare that Goniwe's political ideas first formed. Unlike Steve Biko, he was drawn to Marxism. His group met regularly to share banned books and debate on ideology and governance. But spies were everywhere, and he was arrested in the crackdown after the Soweto Uprising, and with three others, sentenced to jail for promoting communism.

Nyameka had to leave their eight-month-old baby with her mother-in-law to continue with her studies.

In prison, Goniwe had time. He loved to study and enrolled for a postgraduate degree in teaching. He enjoyed reading poetry, especially that of Guy Butler, at that time a professor and head of English at Rhodes University in Grahamstown. He wrote to Butler asking for help with writing poetry. He figured he had nothing to lose anyway. To his surprise Butler replied and thus began an unusual correspondence between the two men. Goniwe's prison walls inspired him to write his poem "These Walls."

Walls, walls, walls.
Walls all around me...
Close, too close
Strong, rigid, firm,
Close, too close,
They explode into my consciousness,
Big, bulking, bold...

After spending four years in prison, in 1982 Goniwe was thrilled to become a father again. They named the baby Nyanisa, meaning to be true or upright.

Soon he was appointed acting headmaster of a school in Cradock. The school was in the heart of the township. Around it, matchbox houses sat like strings of beads on a rosary. Cows wandered across the streets and at night packs of feral dogs roamed the same streets.

Goniwe was horrified at the state of the township. The schools and churches had descended into a moral morass, renting their premises for discos that provided a front for drugs, liquor, and even the rape of young girls.

With a fellow teacher and activist, Fort Calata, Goniwe began a cleanup. They replaced the discos with school concerts and choir practice. At school, Goniwe threw himself into his work. Discipline with empathy remained at the core of his approach. He loved teaching and on weekends taught math and science to struggling students. He enjoyed spending time with his students, and they with him. They looked up to him as their leader, and his commitment to them was unwavering.

He encouraged the students to organize themselves. Under Fort Calata's guidance, the students launched the Cradock Youth Association, which was affiliated with the UDF.

But the police were concerned about the influence Goniwe and Calata wielded in the area. They opened files on the men, whom they classified as "A" activists, or those of highest concern.

The police were correct in being uneasy about

Goniwe. Since his return to Cradock, he had been working actively underground with the ANC. He made trips to neighboring Lesotho to meet with Chris Hani, Umkhonto commissar and ANC underground coordinator. Thus, the embryonic Cradock structures reported through Goniwe and others directly to the ANC in Lusaka.

General van der Westhuizen, commanding officer of the security forces in the Eastern Cape, said later, "Anarchy reigned in certain parts of the Eastern Province... Goniwe played a prominent role in the revolutionary onslaught. He was one of the leaders of the UDF... Furthermore, he was one of the leaders of the militant youth movements of the Eastern Cape region."

It was two in the morning when the police raided Goniwe's house and arrested him. Fort Calata was arrested as well, and all political meetings were banned for three months.

The students marched through town demanding the men's release. Riots broke out, with students firebombing and stoning the homes of community councilors. The police resorted to whipping the students with thick whips made from rhinoceros hides. Eventually the army was brought in, and the township was cordoned off.

Angered by the presence of the army, the community organized a boycott of white-owned shops during June 16. The police used tear gas and batons to disperse the crowd.

Finally, after six months in prison, Matthew and Fort were released.

Still defiant, Matthew called for a "Black Christmas," during which the community would resist buying liquor and food from white-owned shops. They printed posters that read: "Black Christmas: 200 people died this year: 1000s of pupils out of classes: 1000s of workers lost jobs: No Cause to Celebrate."

The call for civil disobedience was heeded by almost everyone far outside Cradock. White shops were virtually empty of customers during one of the busiest times of the year.

Like Steve Biko almost a decade before, Goniwe was also fast becoming a diplomat in waiting. He was interviewed by international newspapers and even met with Senator Edward Kennedy and hosted UDF leaders during their visits to Cradock.

To "neutralize" him, the government arranged to transfer him to a school in a rural area a few hours away.

Students rallied and arranged a boycott which started in Cradock and spread throughout the region. One of the songs students sang was a hymn, "Matthew Somlandela... Matthew Somlandela," meaning "We will follow Matthew... no matter what."

The school boycott evolved into the largest yet seen in the country. Close to seven hundred thousand students heeded the call to boycott, which lasted a year and a half, becoming the longest school boycott in South African history.

In the rest of the country, unrest was spreading like a contagion. Gold miners went on strike for higher wages, a general strike against the use of the army in the townships involved hundreds of thousands of workers, and UDF leaders drew unwelcome international scrutiny of the government by taking refuge in the British consulate in Durban.

In the meantime, the security police tightened their now brazen surveillance of Goniwe and his fellow UDF activists' movements. He was denied the right to own a house by the Lingelihle town council, forcing him and his family to live with his mother-in-law in an extended family home.

The police used their usual tactics to terrify and unnerve the family, including early morning raids, constant surveillance, death threats, phone bugging, short-term detentions for questioning, mysterious phone calls, and tampering with cars.

Soon, Craig Williamson dispatched Lieutenant van Jaarsveld, a member of his intelligence unit, to Cradock, to investigate the possibility of "taking out" Matthew Goniwe.

24

IT WAS ABOUT THIS TIME that I fell in love.

Tired of Johannesburg, I moved to Durban. I disliked the city at first. It has a humid, subtropical climate, which was most unbearable during February, the month I moved. With no air conditioning in my car or in my apartment, for the first time in my life, I discovered I had sweat glands on my upper lip that actually worked. And soon after I moved, I learned my suburb was being terrorized by the Overport rapist. I spent most of my days looking over my shoulder, or stayed indoors with my doors bolted.

Finally, I gathered my courage and attended a political meeting of the Natal Indian Congress. I met a group of young activists. Among them was a tall, soft-spoken guy with large teardrop glasses. He was totally a nerd, but my kind of nerd.

My husband-to-be had recently graduated from the same medical school as Steve Biko. Biko's influence had continued in the years after his death. The student representative council, of which my husband was a member, was a defiant bunch of students prone to challenging their lecturers and to boycott classes frequently.

With an entirely black student body and largely white academics, tensions often ran high. Many of the white lecturers were angry their children had to attend whites-only medical schools elsewhere, where they had to pay fees, which would not be the case if their children were allowed to attend the blacks-only medical school where they themselves taught.

On our first date, my husband and I saw Roger Moore as James Bond in *A View to a Kill*. The opening sequence is breathtaking, with Bond flying on skis through a beautiful snowscape, which was highly unlikely to be in Russia, given the Cold War. He deftly avoids the machine gun fire of an entire Russian squad and then converts the rails of his snowmobile into a snowboard and escapes to the sound of the Beach Boys singing "California Girls." A curious choice, in retrospect.

Years later, I asked my husband what he remembered about our first date.

"I learned something about you that day."

"Uh-huh. What?"

"Well, the movie opens with this cool scene in the snow, and there's two guys in a helicopter talking. You turned to me and said, 'Russians.' And I remember two people in front of us turned around and glared at us. I learned that you like to talk in the movies."

I guess I should have stuck to the lawyer's code of never asking a question you don't know the answer to.

In 1982 the apartheid government had passed the Internal Security Act, which suppressed any actions thought to promote communism, prevented the gathering of people and called for the imprisonment of anyone who challenged the government in any way. It also empowered the President to close any educational institutions if he deemed it a source of unrest.

My doctor, Dr. Essop Jassat, a patron of the UDF, was one of sixteen people arrested and charged with treason under this act. It is strange now, reflecting on those times, at how calmly he and his family accepted the news. It was as if he had no choice but to defy the government, although only he knows the true agony of his imprisonment.

The sixteen spent many months in prison, after which they were eventually released on bail. The trial ran through the first year of my time in Durban, during which I saw my dad frequently, in fact more so than I would have liked, as I was enjoying my new-found freedom from my family.

At the end of lengthy videotape evidence of political rallies, the judge ruled the State had failed to prove violence, revolution and treason, and ordered the accused to be released. The State had however accomplished its purpose—to keep key leaders out of action.

However it had also underestimated the grassroots power of the UDF, which threw up new leaders even as others were jailed, to continue the struggle.

25

In Cradock, the unrest continued unabated. On June 27, 1985, Matthew Goniwe, Fort Calata, Sicelo Mhlawuli, the headmaster of a sister school, and Sparrow Mkhonto, an ex-student of Matthew's, left Port Elizabeth after a UDF meeting. It was late in the evening, and they were headed home because Goniwe felt guilty about not spending enough time with his wife and their children.

Nyameka said, "I had that terrible feeling. A strange feeling... When everyone was asking, 'Did Matthew return?' I went to town... There were rumors emanating from white Cradock that your king is dead."

A heavy silence shrouded Cradock that day.

Nyameka went to the police station to ask if her husband had been arrested. Rebuffed, she returned home to be told the police had called. They left a message with her brother-in-law's young son that Matthew's burned car had been found near the Scribanta Racing Course outside Port Elizabeth.

Two days later, the charred, stabbed remains of Sparrow Mkhonto and Sicele Mhlawuli were discovered a few miles from where the car had been found. The burnt and mutilated bodies of Matthew

Goniwe and Fort Calata were located three days after that.

A few weeks later, thirty-five thousand mourners gathered for the funeral of the Cradock Four. Diplomats from France, Denmark, Sweden, Norway, Australia, and Canada attended. Representatives of the Reagan and Thatcher administrations were conspicuously absent.

For the first time, in open defiance of the police and in a symbolic "unbanning," young activists unfurled the green, black, and gold of the ANC and the red hammer and sickle flag of the South African Communist Party.

The very next day, the government of P. W. Botha declared the first of two states of emergency. Undaunted, the community embarked on a new round of protests.

But with every protest, the government became more desperate. The police targeted the youth in particular. Unlike workers, who had the backing of gigantic unions and leverage brought by their ability to wreak economic turmoil, students had no such protections.

In sweeping raids, five hundred COSAS members were detained over a period of a couple of weeks. The state of emergency was extended to a year, and police were given wide powers to arrest, detain, and interrogate political activists. Most of the students were tortured to reveal the names and locations of their colleagues.

Matthew Goniwe lies buried in Cradock, at the foot of a small hill. By the time of his death, aged thirty-eight, he had headed a movement that liberated

Cradock and inspired millions in the struggle against apartheid. After his release, Nelson Mandela visited the graves of the Cradock Four. He said, "The deaths of these gallant freedom fighters marked a turning point in the history of our struggle. No longer could the regime govern in the old way. They were the true heroes of the struggle."

26

VOLKS HOSPITAL SITS IN THE hollow of a cupped palm, with Table Mountain behind it and the blue Atlantic Ocean in front. Almost every room in the hospital has a view of one or both of these magnificent natural wonders. In summer, the salty breeze from the ocean whispers through the palm trees, which contrast sharply with the gaudy pink bougainvillea flowers that drape the walls.

In early November 1985, a few months after the murder of the Cradock Four, Nelson Mandela was admitted to the hospital. At that time it was a whites-only hospital, but the apartheid government could not risk admitting the world's most famous prisoner to a hospital for blacks, where he would be easily recognized. At least at Volk Hospital there was little chance of this happening.

Like millions of men his age, the sixty-seven-year-old leader was suffering from urinary problems. The prison doctor had diagnosed an enlarged prostate and recommended surgery.

A few days after his surgery Mandela was in his hospital room, admiring the summer sky above Table Mountain, when a nurse ushered in a visitor. In his autobiography, he said, "A surprising, unexpected one. Kobie Coetsee, the minister of justice."

"He was sitting in a chair in the corner in hospital attire, but even that he wore with dignity. I tried my best to create the appearance of an ordinary event," Kobie Coetsee said in an interview years later.

The two men chatted cordially, both pretending that the visit was nothing out of the ordinary. Coetsee said, "We met as though it was not the first meeting... It did not bear the stamp or even appearance of a meeting between... warder and prisoner."

Thus, at the end of 1985, began the tentative "talks about talks" between Mandela and the apartheid government. There was good reason for Coetsee's visit.

In the USSR, Mikhail Gorbachev had been elected general secretary of the Communist Party. His rise and subsequent election as president of his country brought about the implementation of his political reformation, called Perestroika.

With its major enemy now scaling down the Cold War, the US began its own dampening down, and the apartheid government was left without its most powerful backer.

South Africa itself was in chaos.

In Crawford, Cape Town, a coloured township in the Cape Flats, in what came to be known as the Trojan Horse Massacre, police hidden inside crates on a flatbed truck opened fire on youngsters from the Alexander Sinton High School. On that day three young people, aged eleven, thirteen, and twenty-one, were killed and fifteen others injured. The incident was not the first of its kind, but it was the first caught on camera by a CBS news crew. The video went viral, adding impetus to the global anti-apartheid movement.

Elsewhere, workers were uniting. The student movement refused to be crushed, rising like a phoenix in spite of being banned, and thousands of UDF leaders were arrested. The townships were now hotbeds of violence, with open warfare between the government-sponsored Inkatha Freedom Party and UDF supporters.

But the apartheid government was not yet ready for real change.

27

One evening in Stockholm in early 1986, Sweden's Prime Minister Olof Palme was walking home from the cinema with his wife, Lisbet. A week before he had declared, "A system like apartheid cannot be reformed; it can only be abolished." He announced massive increases in aid to the anti-apartheid liberation movement and the widest boycott of South Africa that Sweden had ever undertaken.

It was 11:15 p.m. when they stepped out of the cinema. Palme had given his bodyguards the night off as he wanted to take a walk and stretch his legs. It was cold, their breath came out in white puffs, and their footsteps crunched in the dirty snow.

The couple walked down Sveavägen, a wide, luxury-shopping street. As they reached the intersection with Tunnelgatan a tall man in a black overcoat stepped closer. Seconds later the sharp pop-pop of bullets shattered the evening quiet. The man escaped up the steps on Tunnelgatan and disappeared into the night.

A bullet grazed Lisbet, but Palme was shot in the back at close range. The bullet entered between his shoulder blades and pierced the great vessels near his heart.

He was declared dead soon after arriving at the hospital. Did the apartheid government kill Olof Palme?

We don't know. But in 1996, Eugene de Kock, Craig Williamson's colleague who had traveled to London with him, accused Williamson of being responsible for the assassination.

Williamson repeatedly denied the allegation. The apartheid government denied having agents in Sweden at the time, but six months later a bomb went off in the ANC offices in Stockholm.

Back in South Africa, an estimated ten thousand protesters were detained during the first six months of the state of emergency.

The detentions only served to fuel the protests. The unrest caught both the apartheid government and the ANC off guard. Exiled thousands of miles away in Lusaka, the ANC had no reliable way of knowing what was happening inside the country, much less control events from afar. Thus it was often one step behind the grassroots organizations that made up the UDF.

The ANC itself was split. The hawks were keen to continue the military struggle while the doves were eager to search for a negotiated settlement. The apartheid government's vicious crackdown resulted in the hawks prevailing, even though the ANC stood little chance in winning militarily, given the enormous might of the South African Defence Force, which received a quarter of the national budget.

In 1985, at a tightly controlled conference in Kabwe, Zambia, the ANC's National Executive Committee and delegates, of which the largest voting bloc was the army, agreed to ramp up insurrection within South Africa's borders and took the unprecedented step of eliminating the distinction between "hard" and "soft" targets.

The result was that in 1986 alone there were 230 military operations by the ANC documented within South Africa. The vast majority still involved non-civilian targets like police stations, military barracks or installations, power stations, and railway lines, but increasingly land mines were laid in farm areas along the border, and civilian targets were considered.

On June 14, 1986, two days before the tenth anniversary of the Soweto Uprising, a Saturday, my fiancé and I decided to go to the beachfront. Durban's Golden Mile was a vibrant, popular stretch of beachfront where white-owned restaurants had recently opened their doors to people of color. The promenade, with its man-made piers that separated beaches by race, was a lively place to walk in search of a drink. Our new favorite restaurant was a small bistro next to two bars, Magoo's Bar and the Why Not Bar. Neither of the bars was friendly to blacks, preferred mainly by regulars from Natal Command, the army base located a block away, and the police station nearby.

Unknown to us, at the same time Robert McBride, the twenty-two-year-old coloured commander of an Umkhonto special ops unit in Durban was headed to the same spot we were making for. McBride had been recruited into special ops a year before, and within that time his unit had attacked three electrical substations, a water reservoir, and the homes of at least two collaborators who were standing for office in the sham elections devised by the apartheid government. A few days before that evening in June, McBride returned from Botswana in a car loaded with sixty kilograms of explosives, which he then fitted with detonators and shrapnel. He carefully secured the bomb into the trunk of a blue Ford Cortina.

On a previous occasion he had driven around Natal Command in search of a place to park the car. But the entire block was a strictly guarded no-parking zone. He then chose his "soft" target, right outside the Why Not Bar. He drove the Cortina to the small block of beachfront where we were headed and parked two doors away from the restaurant where we planned on having a late-night dinner.

The bomb exploded around nine-thirty.

We were less than a mile away when we heard the sonic boom of the explosion. Three young women died in the blast, and sixty-nine people were wounded.

Like the people who worked at the Twin Towers and who by sheer chance called in sick for work on 9/11, I often marvel at how we so narrowly missed being killed in that explosion. I know we would have tried to find a parking spot closest to the restaurant. We might even have stopped right next to the blue Cortina.

28

DURBAN'S HARBOR IS THE SECOND busiest in Africa. It handles roughly two thirds of the country's cargo. Its importance to the economy of South Africa is undeniable. In 1986, it was also a key factor in US President, Ronald Reagan's stance on apartheid. In a speech in July of that year, while the Comprehensive Anti-Apartheid Act was being hotly debated in the US Senate, Reagan said, "This is one of the most vital regions of the world. Around the Cape of Good Hope passes the oil of the Persian Gulf, which is indispensable to the industrial economies of Western Europe."

On one end of the crescent that makes up Durban Harbor is Addington Hospital. Situated on prime beachfront property, Addington was for whites only, with a small separate section for coloured patients. The main wards of the hospital were housed in a tall building with almost all rooms having a full view of the Indian Ocean. We, black doctors, were not allowed to rotate through Addington.

A few miles away along the crescent is King Edward VIII Hospital, named after the British monarch who abdicated the throne a week after the opening of the hospital. King Edward was a morose cluster of brick buildings, situated in the midst of the hustle and bustle of taxi ranks and bus stops. Severely underfunded, it served vast areas of the province. Patients were routinely "double-decked," one on the bed, the other on a floor mattress below the bed. During ward rounds, the patient who occupied the bed was asked to vacate it in order to allow us to examine the patient below the bed.

In the pediatric wards fragile newborns shared incubators. Rats were a chronic problem, sometimes so daring as to enter the wards to chew on the fingers or earlobes of sick babies.

I spent much of my time in the Eye Clinic, a brick building the size of a three-bed roomed house. I still remember Eye Clinic's unique smell of fried chicken and body odor as hundreds of patients and their caregivers made their way through its doors. Luckily the examination rooms were air-conditioned, mainly to prevent damage to expensive ophthalmic equipment.

R. K. Khan Hospital in Chatsworth, an Indian suburb of Durban, was another hospital through which black doctors were allowed to rotate.

In 1989, in spite of, or maybe because of, four years of a state of emergency, defiance fever gripped the country. The Mass Democratic Movement, a loose alliance formed after the clampdown on the UDF, called for a Defiance Campaign similar to that which Mandela and his colleagues had conducted in the late 1950s.

At King Edward, many of our African and Indian

patients who were able to leave their beds volunteered to join a march to Addington Hospital. Two thousand medical activists—doctors, nurses, physiotherapists, pharmacists and others—joined the march. We sang freedom songs as we closed off roads with our sheer numbers. Many patients with their drip stands in tow walked the last few blocks to the beachfront.

The massive crowd gathered—in open defiance of the state of emergency as it was illegal to gather in a public place without permission—in front of the hospital entrance, blocking the beachfront area for hours.

Addington Hospital administrators had been warned to admit any patients of color who presented themselves at the door. This they did, but in a separate section of the hospital. And, of course, most of our patients were promptly discharged a few hours later.

Gripped by the same defiance fever I challenged my head of department a few weeks later. I was now in my last years of training and when one of the white registrars reported ill, I was asked to go to Addington Hospital to cover his shift.

I debated it briefly with my husband and then made an appointment to see my Prof.

"I can't go to Addington. If my dad had a heart attack outside that hospital, they would not admit him. I can't go to work there," I said to her, my heart in my throat. I knew my actions could be career suicide but my conscience would not allow me to work at Addington while it was segregated.

I cannot remember every word of our conversation except that it became quite heated with Prof accusing me of being racist for not wanting to treat white patients. I left in abject misery and burst into tears when I saw my husband that evening. I was convinced I would be fired the next day.

However I was not, and nor was I expected to rotate through Addington.

29

It was February 11, 1990, a Sunday. I was sitting in the lounge with my two-year-old son as we watched TV, waiting for Nelson Mandela to be released from prison.

It was a beautiful day there in Cape Town. A few clouds swabbed the summer sky and a breeze from the Atlantic Ocean caressed Table Mountain and fluttered the ANC's green, black, and gold flags held by those gathered to welcome Mandela to freedom.

Wearing a gray suit with a tiny white handkerchief peeping out from his lapel pocket, hand-in-hand with his wife, his other fist held high in the black power salute, Mandela stepped out and smiled.

Over twenty-seven years, while humans traveled to the moon and back, he had seen her for a total of less than two weeks, and his children for no more than a few hours.

"Why are you crying, Mom?" My toddler stared at me with soulful eyes.

"Because I'm happy, Baby," I whispered.

"Welcome to South Africa. Follow the arrows to

arrivals," the immigration officer said to Dee, Tsietsi's younger brother.

He was returning for the first time in fourteen years. In 1976, fifteen-year-old Dee had followed Rocks and Tsietsi into exile. All he wanted was an education. He had been uprooted repeatedly, jostled from Swaziland to Mozambique to Egypt and then finally to SOMAFCO in Tanzania. There he completed his high school education, and with a scholarship from donors he completed a journalism degree.

But his return was a sad occasion. For ten years no one in the family had seen Tsietsi. After graduating from college Dee travelled to Nigeria to find his brother. The man he saw, shrunken and pitiful, was a far cry from the dynamic, lively young man he had once known. The two brothers spent the afternoon together, catching up on old times. But Dee was saddened. Tsietsi struck him as paranoid and illiterate. He had lost his flair for language and literature. Welma had left him after he hit her, taking their two girls with her, and now he was convinced she wanted to kill him.

Dee returned to Tanzania, and again Tsietsi disappeared. Then a few years later their brother Mpho called Dee. "Tsietsi is dead."

It took Dee a few minutes to fully grasp what Mpho was saying. Finally he sat down and wept.

Now, as Dee made his way through immigration, in the hold of the plane was the coffin that bore Tsietsi's remains. Still in his early thirties, Tsietsi had died in Guinea, alone and far from home. The cause of his death was unknown. It was said to be AIDS, but at the funeral home, his body was found to have severe injuries; thus, homicide could not be ruled out. Nomkhitha and Joseph declined an autopsy.

As with so many political funerals of the time, Tsietsi became everybody's brother or son. AZAPO, the organization that saw itself as a direct descendent of Black Consciousness, wrangled over the ceremony with the ANC. Hundreds of youths danced and chanted as their hero was buried. Much later, the family grieved in private.

Tsietsi lies buried in Avalon Cemetery in Soweto, not far from where Hector Pieterson is buried.

And thus an era came to an end. Four cohorts of brave youth moved on into death or adulthood, young people who looked apartheid in the eye and refused to stand down.

Over the decade between the first "talks about talks" between Mandela and Coetsee, until the first democratic elections in 1994, the apartheid government continued to kill thousands as it flailed desperately in its death throes.

When it became obvious that democracy was inevitable, the state went on a massive shredding spree. Almost all evidence of covert activities that could implicate anyone in the apartheid government was shredded, leaving sparse evidence to bring the guilty to justice.

The Truth and Reconciliation Commission was set up under Archbishop Tutu. Unlike other truth commissions, it was a legal body that had powers to subpoena and arrest people who refused to testify. The archbishop said its main aim was "restorative justice" not "retributive justice." To this end people on both sides were encouraged to come forward and tell the whole truth. In return they received amnesty and were protected from extradition on crimes committed on foreign soil.

In a special hearing on children, Max Coleman, whose son's detention prompted him and his wife, Audrey, to take up the cause of children in detention, testified, "At least eighty thousand detentions occurred from 1960 up until 1990, and most of them from 1985 onward." About two thirds of all detainees were younger than twenty-five, and a quarter (about twenty thousand) of all detainees were children under eighteen, many as young as seven. One out of every eight detainees was a woman or a young girl.

Craig Williamson, whose bid in 1987 for office as Member of Parliament for Bryanston was a dismal failure, was subsequently appointed to the President's Council, an advisory body, where he remained until 1991.

After 1994, to avoid extradition, Williamson applied for amnesty. He took full responsibility for only three bombings: Jeanette and Katryn Schoon, Ruth First, and the London ANC offices. He denied any culpability for the murder of Olof Palme and assassinations and bombings in South Africa, Zambia, Sweden, Botswana, and Swaziland.

He was granted amnesty, which meant he could not be extradited for any acts of terror or murder committed outside South Africa.

Soon after, he melted away into the fabric of the new South Africa.

EPILOGUE

WITH THE BIRTH OF DEMOCRACY, the new government was handed a fractured, unequal education system. For many white children, public schools were better than in Europe, but most black children attended derelict schools; libraries were nonexistent, and science labs had to borrow beakers. These problems were compounded by a critical shortage of teachers.

The dreams of millions of black children were in danger, as were those of the parents who had sacrificed their own futures for them.

Fast-forward to today. It's been over twenty years since apartheid ended. The number of black students enrolled at all levels of education has increased dramatically. But dropout rates remain high, and the single largest reason for dropping out of both high school and college is lack of money. The racial divide is still evident, with only three out of a hundred young Africans enrolled in higher education, compared to twenty out of a hundred young whites. The equivalent figure for the United States is approximately forty per hundred.

In October 2015, a government cutback on

university funding resulted in universities raising fees by between 10 and 12 percent. At my alma mater, Wits, hundreds of students, the children of those who fought apartheid decades ago, gathered in the lobby of Senate House, the home of the administration offices.

This time the protests were led by two women, the outgoing student representative body president, Shaeera Kalla, and the incoming president, Nompendulo Mkatshwa. The students invited the vice chancellor to sit down on the floor and chat. To his credit, he did, and he agreed to halt the fee increase. But the Wits protests had already inspired students facing the same issue at other universities. On Twitter, the hashtag #FeesMustFall exploded.

Small Daddy: Tomorrow is D-Day. Sikhathele! #FeesMustFall.

Eyaaz Matwadia: If we don't take a stand... Our futures won't be able to stand #FeesMustFall

Nthabiseng Mazeka: Free quality education in our lifetime #FeesMustFall

The demand spread. Students, many of them likely to graduate with thousands of rands of debt, took to social media and the streets. Slogans such as "If education is the key to the future, you can't hide the key" came to express the students' frustration. Classes ground to a halt.

There is little doubt the ANC-led government has failed the youth of South Africa.

Yes, it inherited a chaotic situation in 1994. It had

to merge nineteen separate departments of educatio into one, and then it had to battle angry white parent who refused to open "their" public schools to black children. Yes, the ousted regime's operatives were estimated to have squirreled away close to $2 billion in offshore accounts. Yes, the ANC struggled against a devastating AIDS epidemic, and yes, it struggled under a global financial crisis of staggering proportions. Finally, yes, the digital revolution created a vast divide between the rich and poor, and in South Africa this generally means white and black.

But it also experimented needlessly with outcomes-based education for close to ten years, leading to what many call the "lost generation." Ex-president Thabo Mbeki's government denied treatment for AIDS to its people, which led to the preventable deaths of millions of parents, teachers and students, and left millions of children orphaned. And most recently, under President Zuma's administration, corruption has flourished, with money diverted away from schools into the pockets of middlemen.

To poor South Africans, the cost of higher education is another obstacle to participating fully and equally in the country's economy.

On October 23, 2015, university students took their fight to the Union Building, the official seat of Zuma's government. Tens of thousands of students marched into Pretoria, as their grandparents had done under apartheid sixty years before.

Businesses provided water and snacks for the crowd, and clergy and supporters marched with the

ʔ But police, continuing their own legacy in .t, fired into the crowd again (this time with bullets, fortunately) to clear the lawns in front e building. Inevitably some students resorted to .ence, though it is rumored these were "outside ements" sent to stoke trouble. Some liquor stores were looted, some police cars set alight. Rocks were hurled at riot police again, and again they retaliated with tear-gas canisters.

In Cape Town, students marched on parliament. As they sang the national anthem, police fired flash grenades.

Nonetheless, that afternoon Zuma announced a moratorium on fee increases. People both celebrated and voiced their reservations on Twitter:

Beyonce Pad Thai: Someone asked me how my day was. I said I'd been tear-gassed and shot at by the government I'd voted for. My heart is sore. #FeesMustFall*

Ba_ntu: this was not a concession by government, rather it was containment. #FeesMustFall

#FeesMustFall is the first step in the ongoing struggle toward an equal education, which remains an unrealized dream in a country where half the nation has no running water in their homes. Although history never repeats itself exactly, it can come close, and the question remains what the students can learn from their predecessors. Whether they can align their struggle with that of their brothers and sisters who are still in school and leverage their power by aligning with other sectors of the communities they live in. Whether they can rally the clergy and their parents to their side. Whether they can shame businesses int investing, really investing, in them and their cause foı the future we all envisaged in 1994.

But more important, the question is whether they can avoid the fate of youth uprisings like those of the Arab Spring where youth played a central role only to be sidelined by their elders. Whether they can stand up to the ANC-led government, the seasoned politicians, who seem to have forgotten why they battled the apartheid government so many years ago.

"At the southern tip of the continent of Africa, a rich reward is in the making... This reward will not be measured in money. Nor in the collective price of the rare metals and precious stones that rest in the bowels of the African soil... It will and must be measured by the happiness and welfare of the children, at once the most vulnerable citizens in any society and the greatest of our treasures.

"The children must, at last, play in the open veld, no longer tortured by the pangs of hunger or ravaged by disease or threatened with the scourge of ignorance, molestation and abuse, and no longer required to engage in deeds whose gravity exceeds the demands of their tender years."

– Nelson Mandela Speech at the Nobel Peace Prize ceremony, 1993

ACKNOWLEDGEMENTS

My deepest thanks to the brave young men and women, and their families, who sacrificed so much for a free South Africa.

I am also grateful to the people whose love and faith made writing this book possible: Ba & Dada who watered me, Paresh - my other half without whom I would be lost, Diptesh, Sejal and now Anna - my muses who keep me young, Deepak and Bhads who kept me grounded, sometimes physically, Mots, my sister, Bengt & Lena whose story sent me down this path, and every one of you, you know who you are, who listened and held my hand when I needed it the most.

Thanks also to Beverly, my friend, my tutor and my critic, Libbetts, Kristin, Wanda, Beth & Ruth, for your readings and your belief in me, to Phil Ribera, Carol Ansel, and Daniel Loedel for your insightful and honest critiques, to John Bond & Whitefox Publishing Services for playing matchmaker and David A. Gee: the world's best cover designer. Thank you all.

Finally, thank you, reader, for reading my debut book. I hope you enjoy it.

– Manju Soni

A NOTE ON SOURCES:

This book is part memoir, and as such much of the source material stems from my own experience while living under apartheid. But the heart and soul of the book are three young men, Steve Biko, Tsietsi Mashinini and Matthew Goniwe, and the roles they played in inspiring the youth movement against apartheid together with an analysis of the movement's contribution to the fall of apartheid. For those sections I have, as far as possible, studied first person sources. For the sections on the apartheid government, and in particular, Craig Williamson's role, I have delved deeply through the transcripts of the submissions made to the South African Truth and Reconciliation Commission, which are available online at the Commission's website. For more detailed sources please feel free to contact me at msoni.author@gmail.com.

www.ingramcontent.com/pod-product-compliance
Lightning Source LLC
Chambersburg PA
CBHW051456050726
47593CB00005B/2099

* 9 7 8 0 9 9 7 7 1 9 6 1 1 *